The Justice Paradigm

The Justice Paradigm

Koran, Social Justice & Scientific Sociology

Muhammed A. Asadi

Writers Club Press
San Jose   New York   Lincoln   Shanghai

The Justice Paradigm
Koran, Social Justice & Scientific Sociology

Writers Club Press
an imprint of iUniverse, Inc.

For information address:
iUniverse, Inc.
5220 S. 16th St., Suite 200
Lincoln, NE 68512
www.iuniverse.com

ISBN: 0-595-20896-7

Printed in the United States of America

Koran: A New History of Sociology

> *"Look at the indicators of God's mercy [in the natural world],*
> *how He gives life to the earth after its death, most surely He will*
> *raise the dead to life again; and He has power over all things*
> *[Koran 30:50]."*

The inspiration provided for social research in the Koran, is the book's emphasis on a critical analysis of ideas and ideology. Ideas and ideology bred in ignorance lead, according to the Koran, to a social order that is contrary to the natural social order determined by the creator. A critical analysis is encouraged by the oft–repeated idea in the Koran that reason, rationality and empirical evidence (Koran 3:190–191), in short the method of science, is supreme in determining the truth, given how the human mind is designed to operate.

The Koran presents itself as a "guide with evidence and a criterion" (Koran 2:185) from the maker of all things to humankind, the bearer of God's trust on earth and maintainers of the "balance" (Koran 55:7–9) that God created. However, in "turning away" from that trust and "falling short" of the balance and "wasting by excess", humanity has created a multitude of social problems, problems that harm society in general and not only those who are directly responsible for them (Koran 8:25). It is not mystical determinism but "social" determinism that the Koran talks about (Koran 30:41). Consistent with this view, the Koran frequently mentions a "path" [*Sabeel* in Arabic] of various social actions leading to ends that are harmful or beneficial. This is somewhat similar to "Path Analysis" used by modern sociologists.

"Behold! In the creation of the heavens and the earth; in the alternation of the night and the day; in the sailing of the ships through the ocean for the benefit of mankind; in the rain which God sends down from the skies; and the life which He gives therewith to an earth that is dead; in the animals of all kinds that he scatters through the earth; in the change of winds and the clouds enslaved between the sky and the earth; –(here) indeed are signs for a discerning people." (Koran 2:164)

My work on the scientific analysis of the Koran started the day I discovered a copy of the English translation of the Koran in my father's closet, in 1984. This passion for blending science and religion and to rationally inquire whether the Koran could be justified in its claim of originating with, "the One who knows the secrets of the heavens and the earth and the secrets of the [collective] minds (Koran 35:38)," led to the compilation of three books: Koran: A Scientific Analysis (1992); The Message of Quran and Islam (1995) and The Unifying Theory of Everything: Koran and Nature's Testimony (2000).

I realized in a manner similar to the evolution of the social sciences from the natural sciences, that if the method of science could be used to scrutinize and analyze the Koran in issues involving processes of nature and the natural world, the same could be applied regarding society. Debate about various social issues is common in the media today and more often than not, "religious" ideas regarding them are scoffed at as being unscientific and primitive. Contrary to this popular view, very early on in my readings of the Koran, I discovered an amazing similarity between modern scientific criteria and the Koran. For example, innovative medical drugs whose "benefits are less than their harmful side effects" are banned from marketing by the *Food and Drug Administration* in the United States. The Koran stated similar criteria as justification for prohibiting alcohol and other intoxicating drugs, centuries earlier:

"They ask you concerning intoxicants and gambling. Say to them, in them are great harms and only some benefits for humankind; But the harm of them is much greater than their usefulness (Koran 2:219)."

My scientific analysis of the Koran continued while attending Southwest Missouri State University, in Springfield, Missouri. I made sure that every scientific paper I wrote, incorporated in it ideas from the Koran related to the topic of research. A few of my professors, who were patient and open–minded regarding my work, realized that agreed upon criteria, i.e. objective standards could be used to debate culture and values, scientifically. Sociologists nowadays almost all recognize this (Babbie 1992) though some "dogmatically" charge their science and in the process lose the essence of the scientific method itself. Thus, their use of the label "science" while abandoning the principles of science can be termed a "religion". Using Weber's terminology, turned on its head, it's like being enchanted by the "disenchantment" of the world. In my studies, I try to take the Koran, and the ideas contained within it, as a system (*deen* in Arabic) and base its examination on the principles of science.

The social "case" of the Koran has been closed prematurely. My web articles and this book, aims to reopen that "case" and to reexamine the charges that have been leveled against this book for centuries.

Consider this small chapter (*Sura*) in the Koran:

"Have you seen the one who consciously denies the system [of the Koran]? It is he who will repel the orphans and will urge not the feeding of the needy. Woe unto those who worship, yet are heedless of the purpose of it; Who would be seen at worship but refuse even small necessities to the needy? (Koran 107:1–7)."

"Have you seen," implies an *empirical* verification of, as the sentence continues, the behavior of those who deny the system of the Koran, and those who don't deny it in public but in essence. As empirical evidence of this statement, consider the fact that over 30,000 children die every day on earth by causes that are preventable (UN Human Development Report 2000). In most instances these casualties result because of non–availability of "basic necessities" because of distribution mismatch, perpetuated by capitalism. Now consider the elite who controls these resources and their "conscious rejection" of the Koranic system of distribution of income, based upon *Zakah*. *Zakah* implies a redistribution of 50% of the surplus of every Muslim that is beyond legitimate need, in the form of a social fund that removes iniquities in wealth distribution in society (Koran 59:7). This percentage is much greater than the 20/20 that the United Nations envisions.

As empirical evidence of the second part consider those that are labeled "Muslims", those who are often "seen" at worship five times a day, but remain ignorant of the social consciousness that prayer is supposed to inculcate in a believer. In many "Muslim" lands people starve or die of pre-ventable causes because "small necessities" aren't available, yet the "Muslim" elites in these countries support a life style more conspicuous than those in most rich industrialized nations.

This was a small example of how the Koran approaches the study of individual and group behavior. Social research through operationalization of concepts, on a local or a global scale can provide for empirical testing of the Koran's statements. By making empirical observation the heart of its conclusions, the Koran encourages value–free positive sociology and acceptance that is based on confirmation (*sadq* in Arabic)and not on unreasoned faith at all. The concept of dogmatic "religion" and "blind faith", as understood by Western, English–speaking people, is completely alien to the Koran.

Following the example of the Koran, Ibn Khaldun (732–808) recog-nized as the founder of Sociology,

> *"Emphasized the necessity of subjecting both social and historical phenomena to scientific and objective analysis. He noted that those phenomena were not the outcome of chance, but were con-trolled by laws of their own, laws that had to be discovered and*

applied in the study of society, civilization and history. He remarked that historians have committed errors in their study of historical events, due to three major factors: (1) Their ignorance of the natures of civilization and people, (2) their bias and prejudice, and (3) their blind acceptance of reports given by others."(Zahoor 1996)

Thirteen centuries before Karl Marx (1818–1887) made a broad statement about religion as the *"opium of the masses"*; the Koran came to an empirical conclusion regarding the "use" of religion by the elite. In the following statement of the Koran, it is clearly stated that religion is used by some groups to further their economic causes:

"Woe to those who write the book with their own hands and then say, "This is from God," that they may exchange it for some miserable economic gain. Woe to them for what their hands do write and woe to them for what they earn therewith (Koran 2:79)."

It is not only the interpretation of 'religion' but the interpretation of 'science' as well, what we call pseudo–science, which can become the 'opium of the masses'

Fourteen centuries before Edward O. Wilson (1929–), working as a Naturalist particularly with ants, arrived at his version of Sociobiology, the Koran contained this statement:

*"There is not an animal on earth nor the birds that fly with their wings, but are **communities** like unto you. We have neglected nothing in the book…" (Koran 6:38)*

All through the Koran, is recognition of sociological factors that keep people away from God and His message. Factors like group–solidarity, tradition, the pride in social position, social stratification etc. Mentioned together with these is the social psychology of those who refuse God and the cultural reasons on why they refuse, as are economic considerations and their effects on behavior and society. Things like "being seduced by the life of the world," "not looking beyond their material existence," "being overly engrossed in their competition for the material goods of this life," "staying away from spending because of an unreasonable fear of poverty" and "circuits of income." Competition, mutual rivalry and pride in possessions are described as motivators for individuals leading to a certain type of social behavior and a society that is contrary to the "ideal–type" desired by the Koran.

Consider this conclusion in the Koran, centuries before Vilfredo Pareto (1848–1923) outlined "elite theory":

> *"Thus are appointed in every city elite ones (Akabir in Arabic) of its malicious folk and they plot therein (Koran 6:123)."*

C. Wright Mills (1916–1962), in his pioneering work, *The Power Elite* (1956), reached a similar conclusion as the Koran that has become the basis of countless sociological studies all across the field, including Urban Sociology. Note that the Koran mentions "every city" and not just one city and that it mentions decisions being made (plotting) by the elite that can have major consequences (see Koran 14:46). Compare what the Koran says to what C. Wright Mills wrote in 1956:

> *"The power elite is composed of men whose positions enable them to transcend the ordinary environment of ordinary men and women: they are in a position to make major decisions having major consequences (Mills 1956:3–4)."*

Thirteen centuries before Emile Durkheim (1858–1917) used the term *Social Fact* to describe the objective realities of society that are external to the individuals, yet directs their behavior, and developed the concept of the *collective conscience*, the Koran concluded:

> *"Thus unto **every nation** have We made their doings seem fair. Then unto their Lord is their return, and He will tell them what they used to do. " (Koran 6:108).*

The Koran mentions an accurate description of life, the life–world (**hayat ud dunya** in Arabic) being similar to a play or a game (**Llaib** in Arabic), in which the actors are busy with "passions, pageantry, mutual

rivalry and boasting among themselves in terms of possessions and progeny" (Koran 57:20). The Koran conceptualized this, at least fourteen centuries before sociologist *Erving Goffman* (1922–1982) popularized a
particular type of *interactionist* model, the *dramaturgical approach* that
takes a similar view of life (Schaefer & Lamm 1998:24).

The Koran mentions the *world's life* and its created culture as an "illusion" (Koran 57:20). An illusion that projects an image of permanence yet
is transitory, and an illusion that directs people to accept something as real,
which in reality is engineered, and unreal. This is similar to *'life–world'* and
its colonization, discussed by Jurgen Habermas (1929–), yet it predates his
work by fourteen centuries. The elite and a state controlled by them thus
emerges as a creator of culture(s) by shaping the 'life–world' of individuals,
projected in the form of a society that best serves their interests.

> *"Illusion is an important device in the arsenal of the masters of*
> *capitalism. Their futures are built almost entirely on illusion: the*
> *illusion of white supremacy, the illusion of democracy, the illusion*
> *of fair and free elections, the illusion of free speech, a free press,*
> *and the illusion of a sound economy." (Chinyelu 1999:62)*

The elite [*akabir* in Arabic] not only creates culture by their control of
the diffusion of ideas in society, by their monopoly over "persuasion
resources", they directly create culture by their design and use of space.
Space, how your cities, your neighborhoods, your organizations are constructed, designed and run all have a close connection to culture(s). City
building needs resources and the elite controls these resources.

"In the history of the world, there has never been a propaganda effort
to match that of advertising in the twentieth century. More thought, more
effort, more money goes into advertising than has ever gone into any other
campaign to change social consciousness (Kilbourne 1999:75)."

By strategically displacing jobs and people and concentrating poverty
in the inner cities, the elite, artificially install and nourish a "street code" A
code that forces people, on a social level to adopt it as the only reality, if

they are to survive. Sociologist Elijah Anderson in his book, *Code of the Street* (1999), states

> *"It is nothing less than the cultural manifestation of persistent urban poverty. It is a mean adaptation to blocked opportunities and profound lack, a grotesque form of coping by young people constantly undermined by a social system that historically has limited their social options and until recently rejected their claims to full citizenship (Anderson 1999:146–147)."*

Those who refuse to be "blinded" by such structural alienation are trapped by "chemical–alienation" through alcohol and drugs that directly produce an illusion of reality. As a result of all this artificially engineered culture, a "real world" much removed from the actual real world is projected. A world that traps people in a cycle from which escape becomes almost impossible. Alienation and anomie are closely linked. In this instant society, we have an *instant* anomie–producing instrument, alcohol.

> *"Their example is as a mirage in a desert. The thirsty one supposes it to be water till he comes unto it and finds nothing...or as shadows upon a sea obscure: there covers them a wave, above which is a wave, above which are clouds; layer upon layer of darkness. When they hold out their hands, they almost cannot see them (Koran 24:39–40)"*

Similar to the "initial conditions" studied by physicists, which led to the evolution of a particular type of universe and the eventual emergence of life, without which the universe would not have resembled what we see today and we wouldn't have been here to see it, the "initial conditions" in society that determine its structure are crucial to understanding the nature of interaction. This is in the tradition of Auguste Comte (1798–1857), the person who coined the term sociology and sought to model the discipline after the physical sciences, particularly physics (social physics).

The "initial conditions" in the physical sciences are mysterious and cannot be explained without reference to a designer, the odds of them occurring by chance equal zero by all real measures. Contrary to this, the intelligently set "initial conditions" that determines the economy and the relationships of production have human social origins and can be studied by historical and comparative analysis.

The scientific system demands replication, verification and falsification, hence empirical analysis should become an important part of any theoretical system. It is through empirical verification that workable theories can be extracted from ones that have at best metaphysical and rhetorical value.

In the last 20 to 30 years as progress has been made in the physical sciences, a hidden order has been revealed in nature. Physicists call this the *Cosmic Code*. It is an intelligently designed, normative order (the values of which can be derived by analogy) written in a language that humanity can understand, the language of mathematics. In attempting to understand this message, of which only a small part has been decoded yet, scientists aim to uncover a grand unifying theory of everything. Newtonian "positive" physics is just a small part of this normative (value) order called the *Theory of Everything*. Once this Cosmic Code is decoded, scientists envision linking all human knowledge together based on it. We will then be able to deduce from it, the natural social order and understand the values based upon which "ideal" human societies can be created in reality, rather than the subjective abstractions that embody Max Weber's (1864–1920)"ideal types".

Contrary to the "natural order" conjectured by Herbert Spencer (1820–1903) in his Social Darwinism, which was natural only to the extent of a reproduction of the "social construction" of a particular type of status quo, the *Theory of Everything* will present objective reality of a normative and positive nature based on the larger scale governance of the universe. It will transcend all societies.

Once this theory is understood, it can be speculated that all other systems of social organization based on inadequate and incomplete knowledge like Capitalism, Socialism, Communism, Anarchism and the other "isms" will become obsolete and outdated.

"Therefore, set your face to the system of Islam. The nature of God based upon which he has natured humankind. There is no altering what God creates. That is the established standard order. However most among humankind understand not (Koran 30:30)."

The Koran is not about "self–righteousness," as writings on what is popularly termed as a "religious" source are often accused of being. Theory and action need to be separated for the purpose of pure research. Thus we need to test the Koran by its claims and not by the actions of those who claim to believe in it or follow it.

Throughout history myths and superstition have so crept under the banner of religion that to believe in God came to be considered childish stupidity by modern literary giants. In the face of such opposition we come across a unique book, the Koran. Not only is the Koran written in the most mathematical/logical of all human languages–Arabic, it is unique in history in that it led to the development of the rules of that language itself.

While Bertrand Russell envisioned creating a logical/mathematical language, the Koran did that factually fourteen centuries back. No other book in the history of the world has "invented" the rules of a language, so to speak, as the Koran did when it gave birth to the rules governing written Arabic. Thus Arabic may be described as the ideal "human" language (based upon Russell's criteria) that comes closest to emulating the mathematical language of the universe, in an objective fashion based on its logical foundations, which even the lay person can understand. We need to ask here, could a man who had no formal schooling, *Muhmmed ibn Abdullah*, and lived fourteen centuries back, have done this?

"Arabic most precise and primitive of the Semitic languages, shows signs of being originally a constructed language. It is built up upon mathematical principles–phenomena not paralleled by any other language." (Cleary 1998).

The description of the natural world in the Koran pre–empts much of today's hard–earned scientific findings (see http://www.rationalreality.com).

Consistent with Karl Popper's *Critical Rationalism*, the Koran offers falsification. As such it challenges people of learning to find fault with it and to falsify it. By discovering the Koran, I had unlocked the key to the reality of my 'life–world' within the context of a natural social order, natured in humankind. Sociobiology and neurology are coming close to confirming the "God" part of the brain, "natured" in humankind (Koran 30:30). We live in exciting times. In the intellectual world, the Koran, the source of Islam, presents itself as a challenge to human explanation.

> *"They only know some appearances of the life–world, yet of the ultimate end they are heedless." (Koran 30:7)*

Bibliography:

Asadi, Muhammed. *Rational Reality (http://www.rationalreality.com)*

Asadi, Muhammed. *The Justice Paradigm (http://www.geocities.com/justiceparadigm).*

Koran: Translated from the Arabic

Babbie, Earl. *The Practice of Social Research. 6th ed. 1992.* Wadsworth Publishing Co. California.

Chinyelu, Mamadou. *Harlem Ain't Nothin' But a Third World Country.* 1999. Mustard Seed Press. New York

Cleary, Thomas. *Koran: The Heart of Islam.* 1998.

Ed. Shafritz & Ott. Editors. *The Classics of Organization Theory.* 2000.

Mills. C Wright. *The Power Elite.* 1956.

Schaefer, Robert T & Lamm Robert P. *Sociology.* 6th ed. New York. McGraw Hill Companies.

Zahoor, Dr. A. *Ibn Khaldun.* [http://users.erols.com/zenithco/khaldun.html] retrieved 10/13/'01

1

Constructing a Global Ghetto: Racism, the West & the "Third World"

Howard Zinn narrates his observation, on his way to England, on the Queen Mary. Here, on a passenger liner, there existed the clearest evidence of an artificially created "Third World", inside the 'First':

> "My air crew sailed to England on the Queen Mary. The elegant passenger liner had been converted into a troop ship. There were 16000 men aboard, and 4000 of them were black. The whites had quarters on the deck and just below the deck. The blacks were housed separately, deep in the holds of the ship, around the engine room, in the darkest dirtiest sections. Meals were taken in four shifts (except for the officers, who ate in prewar Queen Mary style, in a chandeliered ballroom–the war was not being fought to disturb class privilege), and the blacks had to wait until three shifts of whites had finished eating." (Zinn 1990:88)

In the late Middle Ages, different regions of the world were almost equally developed (Alexander 1996:17). Then in a course of a few hundred years, Western economic and political domination in the world led to pockets of development and underdevelopment, wealth and poverty, coexisting in close proximity to each other. A clear pattern emerged on a global and local scale.

The emerging dominant philosophy was capitalism, the driving force of which was competition, based on ideas similar to Social Darwinism. An ideology of superiority emerged within the ruling elite, an idea that led to the patterned underdevelopment of the majority world.

The purpose of this chapter would be to explain qualitatively using historical and comparative analysis, and empirically using existing aggregate data, the cause of unequal development in the world, controlled by a few dominant nation–states. Qualitative analysis would include tracing the development of the ghetto in the United States, in comparison to the globalization of poverty and the development of the "Third" and now the "Fourth" world. It will focus on historical and comparative research.

Quantitative analysis will focus on aggregate census, World Bank and United Nations data to document development indicators that suggest differentials within the United States and between the developed and underdeveloped world.

The nation–state was central to Western economic and political domination (Alexander 1996). Nationalism on a global scale can be compared to racism within states. Both are driven by an ideology that assumes superiority of one group over another. I explain this linkage by comparing the relationship between the West and the "Third World" to the dominant ideology that determines race relations between white and black communities in the United States.

Once the cause of the problem is identified scientifically, solutions can be better focused for equitable development and less isolation of the "Third World". As nations come together and the concept of a nation–state becomes blurred, the barriers within societies that prevent equitable development have to be overcome as well. If they are not overcome, then visible borders are simply replaced by invisible barriers.

Ideas of race superiority, made moral by a 'white' hierarchical religion, became institutionalized in Western culture once Germanic races gained power by overthrowing the Roman Empire and adopting Christianity. By the 1900s, the colonial powers of Europe, together with the U.S, controlled half of the newly discovered areas of the world, and over a third of its population (Delavignette 1964:1).

This idea of superiority led to the "race–specific" Atlantic slave trade in which over 40 million people were killed. A similar idea led to the genocide of the American Indians, over 50 million "savages" were killed by the "civilized" West (Zinn 1990:1). American "National Security" masked by an idea about "our way of life," led to the civilian bombings of Vietnam and Cambodia by orders of Harvard educated elite, killing millions again. South Africa similarly used "national sovereignty," as an excuse to protect its apartheid regime. The fate of the Australian Aborigines[1], persecuted, killed and forced on reservations was another racially motivated, national act, as was the dropping of the atomic bomb on Japan and not on white Germany. "Turning the other cheek", pulling out peacekeepers, and not stopping the genocide when 800,000 *Tutsis* were killed by the *Hutu* militia in Rwanda, at the rate of 10,000 per day, in 1994, provides further evidence of non–Western lives being unimportant, to the elite and their "democratic" system.

Colonization and the artificial drawing of borders displaced and killed millions of poverty stricken people in India. The drawing of arbitrary borders, similar to neighborhood displacement within the developed world, cut the lifelines of many groups and communities. European wars among

---

[1] At the time of European colonization in the 18th century, Aborigines numbered about 1 million. At present, according to the 1986 Census, they number 230,000. Their unemployment rate is over six times (600% greater) than the national average, and the average wage of the Aborigines is half that of the national average wage in Australia [Encyclopaedia Britannica]. From less than 1% before colonization, Caucasian [white] population in Australia has reached 92% [of the 19 million who live there], while the Aborigines have become almost "extinct" [World Almanac and Book of Facts 2000].

themselves, the First and the Second World War similarly destroyed millions and plundered the earth. This is the nature of racism. Under the cloak of nationalism, it has killed and caused suffering to more people in the course of a few hundred years than any other single factor.

Terms and their use:

Let me clarify my use of the word "West" and "Third World" in this chapter. When I say "West", I mean the white–male elite, (of European origin) who command decisions in the world (Mills 1956) and not the masses of the white world. Contrary to that, when "Third World" is mentioned, the masses are referred to and not the elite that supposedly rule over these countries. The elite in most of these countries are a part of the "second–tier" West, a legacy of colonialism, intermediaries that translate the Western cause in perpetuating "Third World" Poverty. They are as far removed from their people as the culture of the ghetto is from suburban America.

"Internal Colonialism" signifies the network of *"coercive legal, political and economic constrains imposed on racial ethnic minorities and indigenous peoples in settler societies.… Key to internal colonialism is a set of features that facilitate the exploitation of minorities as workers–segmented labor markets, separate wage scales and state and employer–imposed discriminatory practices"* (Ed. Stasiulis et al 1995:12). It operates within communities just like neo–colonialism operates on a global scale.

Theoretical Background:

The "West" (also called the North or the "core"[2]), traditionally signified European Christian nations. The term nowadays has expanded to include the United States, the industrial states of Western Europe and Japan. Until 1990, the Soviet Union and its Eastern European colonies were excluded

---

[2] According to Wallerstein's *World Systems Theory*, the West or the "core" forces unequal political and economic opportunity on the poor nations of Asia, Africa and Latin America, the "periphery" (Schaefer & Lamm 1998:257)

from the "First World" and became an intermediate division. The term "Third World"(also called the South or the periphery) was invented to signify underprivileged countries, mainly Asian and African, as against the first two (Fieldhouse 1999).

Wallerstein (1974) the person who first formulated the *World Systems Theory*, suggested that since the 16th century, with the rise of capitalism, the world market was purposefully transformed into a group of core countries (those who were former colonizers and who control capital and material wealth in the world) and a set of peripheral countries (the rest of the world). Until Japan entered the group of core nations recently, white male elite controlled the world almost exclusively, in the postcolonial era as they did in colonial times.

The peripheral countries in order to become part of the global economic system, which was deliberately designed to serve the core nations, had to become dependant on them and their provision of developmental resources. The core exploits the periphery for cheap resources, which are exchanged for either expensive military goods or overpriced capital. Political instability and poverty is concentrated in the periphery to keep this global order intact. This ensures that the periphery remains in its subordinate position. In short, this was the reason for the birth of a few affluent nations, controlled by white male elite, surrounded by a poverty stricken "Third World", a world where almost everyone is non–white.

The World Systems Theory can be extended to include segregation and sub–urbanization within the United States as well. In the U.S from 1920 through the 1960s, sub–urbanization continued unabated (Weeks 2000:419), America is now predominantly suburban and the suburbs are predominantly white. Suburbs are the "core" where edge cities have led to the replacement of the central city's dominant position. The central city has become the periphery where minorities, especially African Americans are concentrated. This has led to the development of the ghetto and the birth of the "underclass."

In recent times, with the rise of the so–called Asian Tigers and the oil rich countries of the Middle East, a new group, the "semi–peripheral" countries have entered the World System. These countries are linked to the core but have loose (mostly labor) connections with the majority "peripheral" world. They are part of what Marx would call the petty bourgeoisie. They serve the core in keeping the periphery poor, having aspirations of entering the "core" status by such service. A similar phenomenon was seen in the development of the ghetto in the United States. Massey and Denton (1993) state:

> *"The rise of the ghetto, more than anything else, brought about the eclipse of the old elite of integrationist blacks who dominated African American affairs in the northern cities before 1910...the (profit) interest of these "New Negroes" economic and political leaders were tied to the ghetto and its concerns. " (Massey & Denton 1993:40)*

This hierarchical classification signifies a grouping of states that are similar to each other and superior to the countries beneath them, the "Third World" countries. The "West" or the "First World" is similar in terms of the Christian religion and being white (for the most part), and the "Third World" is predominantly non–white and thus considered inferior and uncivilized. It is implicitly acknowledged and "politely" enforced by the West that white Christian nations are superior to all others and so are God–appointed leaders, *"the white man's burden"*. This ideology has its history in the fall of the Roman Empire, and the subsequent success Europeans had in dividing the world among themselves. The moral justification to subjugate people was provided by the Bible.

Max Weber stated:

> *Behind all ethnic diversities, there is somehow naturally the notion of a 'chosen people'...the idea of a chosen people derives its popularity from the fact that it can be claimed to an equal degree*

*by any and every member of the mutually despising groups (Ed.
Vanhorne 1997:116)*

Recognizing this group tendency, the elite exploited it through moral
reinforcement, which over time became "institutionalized" in Western
thought, to an extent that in modern times it has become an almost
unconscious group response. Carl Jung, the analytical psychologist,
described it as the "Collective unconscious". Cultural transmission by the
West, through its export of media, to the "Third World", has ensured that
this idea of superiority of the West gains acceptance among the poor
masses in the "Third World" as well[3]. The most effective "power" is the
one where the oppressor can get the oppressed to voluntarily work for
their advantage through institutional legitimization. Thus the oppressed
deem that they are doing 'good' even though they are working against
their own interests. The Koran accurately described such "social construction" of reality centuries back:

> *"[Can anyone be more misled] than them, the harmful nature of
> whose deeds is made fair–seeming to them so that they deem them
> good (Koran 35:8)."*

According to this Western ideology, all non–white races (as such the
"Third World") are inferior and need to be led, controlled and kept in
servitude. Civil rights legislation that attacks the effects of such prejudice
and not the cause, have thus failed to significantly alter race relations in
the world. The example of America should suffice as evidence. Except for

---

[3] The influence of the media is illustrated in a recent study done in Fiji. Within three
years of the introduction of television in 1995 to the island, the number of female
teenagers at risk of eating disorders nearly doubled. The "thin is sexy" image presented by
the American media, made those who watched television heavily, 50% more likely to
describe themselves as fat and 30% more likely to diet than those who watched it mod-
erately (Kilbourne 1999:135). Thus the cultural ideal, for a woman, that had existed for
centuries changed, following after a "superior" West.

an extremely small group of elite African Americans (the "semi–periphery"), most have not gained from nearly half a century of legislation–based solutions. Problems perpetuated by ideology require a shift in ideology, without which all legislation is bound to fail.

"Third World" & the Underclass:

The ideology that led to the invention of the term "Third World" similarly led to the invention of the term 'underclass' in America; a nation otherwise advertised as "classless" (Hadjor 1993:129). The underclass described by the conservative section of society signifies a group completely removed from mainstream America. Here alien and "odd" norms prevail, similar to "Third World" culture, which to many conservatives threatens what is described as "our way of life".

According to them, the members of the "underclass" have a "foreign" or "alien" family structure (*The Moynihan Report*) with a 'backward' code of the streets, far removed from the "normal" American "way of life". Their language is as "foreign" as Arabic or other "Third World" languages. It is seen as a section of society where chronic poverty, homelessness, crime, drugs, and disease have reached epidemic proportions, similar to and sometimes worse than the "Third World"[4]. The people living in such a section of society are not termed "aliens" like people from the "Third World" but are completely *alienated* from the outside world, like the "Third World" and its problems from the affluent West, and the outside world is completely alienated from them.

If anyone from this part of society were to go to the 'outside' world, to one of the big shopping malls in the affluent white suburbs, 'polite' racism and what can be called "conspicuous supervision" will keep him/her out of public areas. Access is restricted and clearly marked by "borders" of tolerance, similar to borders that separate nations. A few decades back, borders

---

[4] The New England Journal of Medicine (January 18, 1990, Vol322, No3, p.176) reported that "Death rates for those between the ages of 5 and 65 were worse in Harlem than in Bangladesh." (As quoted by Chinyelu 1999: 1)

were physically marked by "red–lines" on bank maps. Today, those paper maps have been replaced by "mental mapping". Bank statistics, in poor neighborhoods reveals that red lining is still alive and well.

"Racial profiling" ensures that these borders are respected and crossing them can lead to swift "justice", like countless "Rodney King" cases, all through the nation. Similarly, for the "Third World", strict visa and immigration laws, to keep the "barbarians" from reaching "the gate", deportations, detaining people on 'secret–evidence' and 'swift–justice' against 'rogue nations' like Libya, Iraq and Afghanistan, ensures much the same. National security is used as an excuse to curb the de–jure civil rights of minorities and to militarily solve economic problems that threaten the hegemony of the core.

The capitalist elite, the owners of tobacco and alcohol industries, collectively kill over 450,000 American and millions more around the world, every year, yet the system doesn't declare "war" on them.

The appearance and incidence of the geographic region inhabited by the 'underclass' has become an ecological pattern, being found in all major cities in the United States, in contrast to the affluent white suburbs. This is alarmingly similar to the incidence and appearance of poverty in the "Third World" compared to the affluent white "settler societies" like Australia, Canada etc. These areas once used to be prosperous business districts and now are urban wastelands like the "Third World" after colonization, due to strategic population and job displacement.

It is a section of society where informal laws bar its assimilation with the mainstream economy on equal terms. The most one can expect is to get a low–paying service job with a similar entry and exit level, when the economy is good, just as the forced–exchange of manufactured goods for scarce raw materials with the "Third World". If the person is lucky, he/she will keep the job at the same level and not face unemployment, debt, homelessness and starvation. In the case of the "Third World", the most that can be expected is the refinancing of debt owed to the West. With multiple digit inflation and unemployment, even keeping at the same level becomes a challenge that is never met.

It is a section where the majorities, if not all the people are non–white (like the "Third World"). An area, the rest of 'civilized' society wants to be separated and protected from, thus leading to brutal policing similar to the "terrorism" hypes that make the West, militarily police and economically sanction "rogue nations". The area being talked about is very close to home in urban America. It is the American ghetto. A classic "Third–World" nation within the wealthiest country in the world.

The Roots of Racism in Western Thought:

> "The Holy Bible in the White man's hands and his interpretations of it, have been the greatest ideological weapon for enslaving millions of non–white human beings (Malcolm X, as quoted by Alex Haley (1973:241–242)."

Christianity, to the European colonials, together with Biblical passages promoting the mass destruction of "foreign", "heathen" and "strange" elements, gave moral justification to the systematic genocide of millions of non–white people throughout the colonial era. Many lands were claimed, before even setting foot on the shore, *In the name of the Father, Son and the Holy Ghost (Carlyle 1918)."* The propagation of Christianity became the cloak under which pillage and plunder was justified and exonerated. Later, especially by England, it was used to pacify the colonized masses ("give the coat and the cloak"–and then some), by wholesale, metropolitan export of Christian missionaries. The missionaries, themselves under the influence of this superiority complex, employed the tactics of showing the natives their 'superior' Christian religion, based on a 'superior' man–god, Jesus.Martin Bernal, writing about the history of racism states:

> *Racism of the modern type only began in the 15th century, when Portuguese ships began to outflank Islamic power by sailing around the coast of West Africa. They started kidnapping anyone they could find and taking them back to Portugal to sell as slaves.*

Their justification for this was that they were prisoners of a just war, and any war fought by Christians against non–Christians qualified as a just war. Quite soon however a new justification grew up...Africans were claimed to be slavish by nature...The new racists tried to enlist religious backing for their ideological requirements..(Ed. Vanhorne 1997:83)

Since the 1630s in America, a small elite has been manufacturing and reinforcing ideas of "God–given", innate, white racial superiority. This 'power–elite' ensured the socialization of these ideas via the clergy, the intellectuals, the politicians, the academics and the missionaries, all competing for the 'souls' of humanity. Racism thus became a 'religious institution' in America (Griffin 1999:125). Justification in the logic or the pseudo–science of 'color superiority' collapsed over time; the only vehicle that remained to carry it to the present generation was the Bible which was extremely flexible to incorporating the doctrine of innate superiority based on the "chosen" status of the Jewish people presented in the Old Testament.

The relationship between the use by the elite of Christianity and the subjugation of African Americans was well understood by Malcolm X:

"The greatest miracle Christianity has achieved in America is that the black man in white Christian hands has not grown violent. It is a miracle that 22 million black people [now over 30 million] have not risen up against their oppressors—in which they would have been justified by all moral criteria, and even by the democratic tradition! It is a miracle that a nation of black people has so fervently continued to believe in a "turn–the–other–cheek" and "heaven–for–you–after–you–die" philosophy (Haley 1973)."

The Koran, fourteen centuries back, described the use of pseudo–religion by the elite to further their economic desires:

"Woe to those who write the book with their own hands and then say, "This is from God," that they may exchange it for some

miserable economic gain. Woe to them for what their hands do write and woe to them for what they earn therewith (Koran 2:79)."

The forced institutionalization of racism through Christianity by the white elite shows up in the distortion of facts for the purpose of indoctrination and the subsequent labels that survive to the present day. *Labeling Theory* suggests that certain groups in society acquire the power to assign labels to groups. Those labels are then adopted and they might become "self–fulfilling prophecies" of behavior (Schaefer 1998:199). As a result, derogatory labels "invented" by the West and the white–elite survive to this day and are used by members belonging to the oppressed group, almost unconsciously. In America, the Indians who were slaughtered by the millions, got labeled as 'savages' while the settlers became the 'Founding Fathers' and claimants to being 'the most civilized nation on earth.'

Ex–slave, Fredrick Douglas, on a Fourth of July speech to a white audience in 1852 stated about the "democracy"of the elite:

"The rich inheritance of justice, liberty, prosperity and independence, bequeathed by your fathers, is shared by you, not by me. The sunlight that brought light and healing to you has brought stripes and death to me. This Fourth of July is yours, not mine. You may rejoice, I must mourn (Zinn 1990:232)."

The fifty–five *men*, who drew up the Constitution of the United States, were undemocratically picked. There was no representation of over half of the population that were women and over a fifth of the population that were African Americans. Further there was no representation by American Indians, whose land was forcibly taken, in drawing up this document. The roots of what the capitalist elite describe as the "greatest" democracy on earth, therefore are itself undemocratic (Zinn 1990:234). Religion and politics both act as a "tool" of the elite. The constitution itself becomes meaningless to them when it interferes with their economic objectives. Cloaked under the rhetoric of "national security", it is painlessly cast aside. Fear mongering among the masses and the "illusions of fear" spread by their media, act as a catalyst in such efforts to "hijack" the constitution itself.

Max Weber in his writings on power and opposition implies that it would be very difficult (and expensive) for a group to embark on a continuous struggle to control others. If however the position of that group can be institutionalized, opposition becomes muted. Religion served as a vehicle to institutionalize racism. Political scientist, Clarence Stone calls this type of power to institutionalize a group's advantages, *ecological power* (Abrahamson 1996:27).

> *"And thus are appointed, in every city, elite ones of its malicious people, and they plot therein…. (Koran 6:123)*

Vilfredo Pareto outlined "elite theory" (centuries after the Koran), inspired by whom, sociologist C. Wright Mills, did his pioneering work, *The Power Elite (1956)*. Mills states:

> *"The power elite is composed of men whose positions enable them to transcend the ordinary environments of ordinary men and women: they are in positions to make decisions having major consequences (Mills 1956:3–4)."*

The elite targets their "persuasion" resources specifically towards existing influential institutions, for greater impact. Where religion is influential, the elite use it to legitimize their benefits, sometimes politically institutionalizing a distorted version of it. When Paul politically "Romanized" Christianity by bringing into it concepts of "man–god", "son of God" and "Trinity"etc, membership into this "new" version of Christianity increased but it lost the radical "non–elite" reform goal that Jesus envisioned. Jesus himself was a radical reformer. His actions in the temple with the moneychangers (The Bible, New Testament, Mark 11:14–16) shows that he was well aware of economic exploitation.

With Paul however, not only did membership increase but internal strife and factionalism increased as well. This is exactly what *Social Movement Theory* (Collective Identity) would predict happens with an "inclusive" ideological shift (Stoecker 1995). Something similar happened to Islam, two hundred years after Muhammad's death. *Hadith* and other literature were deceitfully introduced as competing canons to the Koran, to boost numbers by making doctrine "inclusive", against the doctrinal "exclusiveness" of the Koran, which resulted in fragmentation and strife, injustice and the replacement of the original goal of universal justice with imperial designs. In small segments, due to such a doctrinal shift away from the Koran, pockets of an oppositional culture were born. Similar to the "code of the street" that leads to inner–city crime, this "code of terror", leads to terrorism. Street crime and terrorism are the offspring of an elite manipulated social and world system. There has been no police solution to inner city crime, similarly there can be no "military" solution to terrorism.

The culture of the elite and the structures created by such a culture are projected upon society in a contradictory manner in order to "legitimize" the norms that help maintain the status quo (Castells 1987:184). Poverty, prostitution and delinquency are structurally perpetuated and implicitly encouraged to display to the masses the consequences of an "alternative" culture. Control of the media and superior access to the masses, by such control of information technology, ensures socialization of this "created" culture. Alienation is unavoidable in such a system.

By strategically displacing jobs and people and concentrating poverty in the inner cities, the elite nourish a "street code", a code that forces people on a social level to adopt it, if they are to survive. Elijah Anderson in his book, *Code of the Street* (1999), states

> *"It is nothing less than the cultural manifestation of persistent urban poverty. It is a mean adaptation to blocked opportunities and profound lack, a grotesque form of coping by young people constantly undermined by a social system that historically has*

limited their social options and until recently rejected their claims to full citizenship (Anderson 1999:146–147)."

Those who refuse this subjugation through this "structural" alienation are offered "chemical alienation" through alcohol and drugs[5], which chemically produce temporary bouts of "anomie", i.e. normlessness and alienation[6]. As a result of this "created" culture, a "real world" much removed from the actual real world is projected. A world that traps people in a cycle, the so–called "culture of poverty", from which escape becomes almost impossible:

> *"Their example is as a mirage in a desert. The thirsty one supposes it to be water till he comes unto it and finds nothing… or as shadows upon a sea obscure: there covers them a wave, above which is a wave, above which are clouds; layer upon layer of darkness. When they hold out their hands, they almost cannot see them (Koran 24:39–40)"*

This is the reality of existence for a majority of humankind. What we consider "real" and "natural" are at times artificially engineered and socially constructed illusions, perpetuated by institutions designed by the elite to serve their economic and political aims.

Alexander (1996) notes:

> *"The most important decisions in the world are made by relatively few people—the top echelons of a dozen ruling parties, a few hundred massive corporations and finance companies. They in*

---

[5] Surprisingly, the Bible contains the same advice for subjugating people:

> *"Give strong drink to him who is ready to perish and wine to those that are heavy of heart. Let him drink and forget his poverty and remember his misery no more (Proverbs 31:6-7)."*

[6] The use of alcohol to subjugate Africans and for acquiring slaves by the colonials, and for the subjugation of American Indians by the settlers is well documented. Alcohol chemically targets the specific area of the brain involved in social control, producing normlessness and alienation, alarmingly similar to what the French sociologist, Durkheim conceptualized as "anomie."

turn are served–and influenced–by senior civil servants, policy analysts, editors and a few thousand lobbyists, pressure groups and think tanks…less than 0.03% of the people in the West. Each country has a different power structure…but their elites have more in common with each other than with their fellow citizens (1996:209)."

Similar to the 'liberation' of the colonies, the 'liberation' of slaves in America was accomplished because it was economically 'useful' to the white male elite in the North. "Chattel" slavery and indentured servitude, was replaced by "wage" slavery for blacks and poor whites, which continues to this day among the masses. "Wage" slavery results in a bigger market and greater profits for capitalists than does "Chattel" slavery.

Talking to a delegation of freed blacks, Lincoln, who is widely proclaimed for abolishing slavery, stated:

"On this broad continent, not a single man of your race is made the equal of a single man of ours (as quoted by Alexander 1996:52)."

Since African American life is "cheap" to the elite (similar to the lives of the masses in the "Third World"), they are welcomed to join the Army and fight America's wars. Among all American casualties in Vietnam, 25% were African American compared to their population of 11% at that time (Alexander 1996).

This "dehumanizing" of African Americans began with European voyagers traveling to Africa in the 16th century. They observed, what according to them seemed like 'pathologies' of Africans. Richard Hakluyt, an early English historian wrote:

"They (the Africans) are black, beastly, mysterious, heathenish, libidinous, evil, lazy and smelly people who are strangely different to our superior white race." (as quoted by Griffin 1999:14)

How the same images are perpetuated even today, is witnessed in so called "government studies". President Nixon's appointed chair of the

"Model Cities Program," commented on the "lower class" city dwellers, who were predominantly black:

> *"The lower class individual lives from moment to moment…impulse governs his behavior. He is therefore radically improvident. Whatever he can't use immediately, he considers valueless. His bodily needs (especially for sex) and his taste for action take precedence over everything else…He works only as he must to stay alive…"(as quoted by Griffin 1999:74)*

It is as if Hakluyt had been resurrected. If we replace the word, "lower–class" with "African", the two descriptions are almost identical. A clarification needs to be made at this point about the "family structure" of African Americans. It is true that single parent, female–headed households are a big problem in African American communities, but the growth rate of "new" cases is lower for African Americans than for white communities (Smith 1998). Whereas the break–up of the family, in the case of African Americans was a direct legacy of slavery, the breakup of the white family may be attributed to a careless attitude towards sex and marriage, the "popular" culture of the "Hollywood" elite. Thus the "morality" issue is forcibly imposed on African Americans instead of on the white 'moral majority'.

> *"The red stain of bastardy, which two centuries of systematic legal defilement of Negro women had stamped upon his race, meant not only the loss of ancient African chastity, but also the hereditary weight of a mass of corruption from white adulterers, threatening almost the obliteration of the Negro home (W.E.B Dubois 1903: 50)."*

Ronald Reagan, one of the most popular presidents in recent history, is well known for his ideological battle with the African American minority. Blaming the poorest, most powerless sections of society for its greatest evils, he drastically cut government funding in public services in the inner cities, leading to a sharp jump in homelessness, inner city riots and brutal police crackdowns. In the "Obi wan" style, Regan, based on his white

Christian 'superiority' ideology went so far as calling the Soviet Union an "evil" empire, and used the medieval term "Barbarians" to describe Arabs and Muslims (Heinman 1998:145).

In 1854 Josiah Nott published a book, in which he claimed, based on his pseudo–science, that Caucasians (White) races have the largest brains and the most powerful intellect (Griffin 1999:51). Following in the same tradition, Charles Murray and Richard Herrnstein authored, *"The Bell Curve: Intelligence and Class Struggle in American Life* (1994)", a few years back. In the book they 'prove' that African Americans are innately (bio-logically)'less–intelligent' than White Americans and as such are destined to a life of crime and poverty, the 'underclass'. They should therefore be controlled by a police state while "the rest of America goes about its busi-ness."(Herrnstein & Murray 1994)

Apart from the fact that Herrnstein and Murray don't have much knowledge of biology, their ideologically manipulated data, comparing IQ to socioeconomic status, has been widely criticized. Ignoring the social legacy of slavery and the subsequent discrimination against blacks as being causal variables, they conclude that innate (biological) intelligence is the cause. This is based on weak correlation of 0.1 (a strong case cannot be made for causation based on correlation alone, especially weak correla-tion). The cultural bias in the IQ test itself is conveniently ignored (Ed. Fraser 1994), as are the over–time increasing "group" IQ scores interna-tionally and even locally among immigrant groups. It is beyond the scope of this chapter to go into details with the 'implicit' racism of Murray and Herrnstein, however it is worth mentioning that if such be the acts of 'intelligent' beings, like the whole sale genocide of communities, the 'less intelligent' animal kingdom shows a lot more prudence in its existence. Controlling for factors like "human interference", the animal kingdom might even outlive 'intelligent' humanity.

It can be argued that the cumulative "implicit" cost of the "superior" final product that capitalists so often "preach" about is much higher (due to the wasted resources of all the competitors who were "killed" along the way) than the "inferior" product of a non–competitive system. By literally "squeezing" the life out of the earth, and leading it towards a premature death, capitalism shows a tendency of not being able to sacrifice the present for the future. The conservative right (the torchbearers of capitalism, the likes of Murray & Herrnstein) however, blames the "underclass" for a similar trait (not sacrificing the present for the future). This makes us wonder who the real source of such a "culture of poverty" is. A source that is similar to the one that installs the "code of the street" and the "culture of terror".

Colonization: The "Third World" developed the West:

Due to the nature of this paper, the historical formation of the "Third World" will not be traced in detail, however major features that led to the persistence of poverty, and the permanence of the "ghetto" will be discussed briefly. The "Third–World" directly led to the development of the West that we see today and the West directly led to the persistence of poverty in the "Third–World". This claim will be substantiated in the paragraphs to follow.

Analysis of the poor in the United States, reveals the dynamic nature of the group. People keep entering and exiting from the ranks of the poor. The one thing that remains consistent is that the majority of the "persistently poor" in the US are the African Americans. Sociologist Herbert Gans, theorized that poverty is deliberately perpetuated in society among certain segments because the poverty of those segments benefits the elite (Gans 1995:91–102). Here on a local and global scale is empirical evidence for Gans' theory:

The American Ghetto: In the late 1940s and 1950s due to economic prosperity, men and women started marrying early and home construction in the suburbs reached an all time high. Middle class white Americans deserted the inner cities in great numbers, as a result by 1970 suburban residents were a majority in metropolitan USA, while before they had been one third of all metropolitan residents. American cities were being rapidly transformed, but one feature of them remained the same and that was the black ghetto. White suburbanization and black in–migration to the north led to an increase in the size of the ghetto. Neighborhood racial turnover was carried out in an almost automatic manner based on what sociologists referred to as the "threshold of white tolerance". A few black families would enter the neighborhood and white residents would start abandoning and selling their homes and moving out. Realtors played a major role in lowering this threshold and made big money in the process. This was achieved by what is called "block busting." Agents would go door to door warning white residents of the "invasion" by black folk. They would purchase the home for a low price, divide it up into smaller units and sell at a premium to black settlers.

As a result of this, spatial isolation segregation indices in the northern cities peaked in the 1950s. In the 1970s the average segregation index for African Americans was 70. This means that 70 percent of blacks would have to move out of a neighborhood in order to achieve an even white black population configuration. In most big cities the number was close to 90 percent. The highest segregation index ever recorded for immigrant groups in the US was 56 for Milwaukee–Italians in 1910. By 1970, the lowest index of segregation for African Americans was 56 in San Francisco (Massey & Denton 1996).

The US federal government was directly involved in the segregation process. To increase employment in the construction industry and increase home ownership, the Home Owners Loan Corporation (HOLC) was started. The HOLC initiated the process of redlining. Those who resided in the redlined areas almost never got loans and could never move out. How the World Bank and the IMF divides up countries of the world into zones and ratings is alarmingly similar to HOLC practices.

By giving a twenty five to thirty five year loan with a 90% guaranteed collateral payment, the FHA (Federal Housing Administration) and VA (Veteran's Administration), during the 1950s and 1960s, encouraged selective out–migration of middle class whites to the suburbs, leading to a decline in the economic base of the city and the expansion of the ghetto. In giving out loans, the FHA determined minimum eligibility requirements for lot size, which effectively eliminated inner city homes, thus forcing those who had got the loan to move out.

Black migration to U.S northern cities during the early 1900s related inversely with the ebb and flow of European migration. When the economy in Europe was booming, European immigrants would move back home creating a shortage of labor in the North. This would boost black migration to the North. In bad times, the inverse would happen. Blacks were also not allowed membership in white unions and as such were used as 'strike breakers' by employers. As the numbers of black migrants increased in northern cities, institutionalized methods were adopted to check the expansion of black settlements. These methods, like red lining, zoning, legalized violence, private contracts etc., made sure that African American populations got concentrated in "ghettos" that were homogeneous, and completely isolated from the main economy (Massey & Denton 1996:31–35).

The similarity between the creation of the ghetto in America and the creation of the "Third World" cannot be overlooked:

1. Colonial powers established trading systems in the colonies to extract much needed resources for the West. These trading systems were controlled by the colonial powers in the case of the "Third World". Higher–level employment was not offered to locals and so there was little transfer of skill (Fieldhouse 1999). This led to "skill mismatch"; similar to what William Julius Wilson discusses as one of the reasons for the development of the "underclass."(Wilson 1996)

2. The primary commodities, and raw materials towards which the "Third–World" economy was forcibly geared were very vulnerable to price fluctuations. This led to the development of a "cyclical"

pattern of poverty, similar to the "ebb and flow" leading to black employment in the northern United States, discussed above. The West even today, allows migrant workers when there is a demand at home and expels them when the economy goes down (Alexander 1996).

> *For 162 years, the Naturalization Law, while allowing various European or "white" ethnic groups to enter the United States and acquire citizenship, specifically denied citizenship to other groups on a racial basis (Takaki 1982).*

3. The local market was forcibly opened to imports of colonial "core–country" products to boost the colonial power's economy thereby destroying the "infant" industries of the "Third World". This is alarmingly similar to the relocation of inner city jobs in America to its white suburbia and the creation of empowerment zones in the inner cities. The zones bring in outside firms that put the local vendors out of business. The big outside firms, at best provide a handful of minimum wage jobs to the community, but drain the billions in purchasing power already possessed by it (Chinyelu 1999).

4. Marketing boards controlled by the colonial powers were set up in these countries and they purchased local produce at prices well below the market, added their markups and sold them to the colonial "core" power. The huge profits they earned were sent to their homes in these "core" countries and not invested in the "Third World" (Fieldhouse 1999). This is very similar to the lack of investment in inner–city infrastructure and employment base building. In most cases, the investment goes to boost tourism and to develop the downtown area, with no money being spent on providing much needed housing and jobs.

5. Currencies of the "Third World" were devalued by force, thus increasing land depletion (desertification) to meet the increased

quantity demanded by the "artificially" lowered price. The extra income and profits were either spent on giving big salaries to the European "managers" of these colonies, or the European owned transportation networks, or the European owned marketing boards. Eventually, all this capital was drained from the "Third World" as these Europeans sent the money back home.

Environmental degradation is not only perpetuated in the "Third World" by the West, minorities face similar environments within the rich industrial countries as well. The US General Accounting Office study of hazardous waste landfill siting found a strong relationship between the siting of offsite hazardous–waste landfills and race and socioeconomic status of the communities in which they were located (Bullard 2000:32)

6. Just like the ghetto, the "Third World" economy was completely detached from the one section of its developed economy that serviced exports to the European colonial powers.

The "Third World" led to the development of the West via (Alexander 1996):

1. Under priced raw materials, and the vast capital flows from the "Third World" sustained Europe during the 19th century and led directly to its modern industrial development.

2. Mineral wealth and Gold extracted from the "Third World" laid the foundation of the capital markets in the West.

3. Over 20 million unpaid Africans forcibly enslaved, added to the surplus that drove the industrial engine.

4. Millions of indentured servants provided labor at wages well below subsistence.

5. Markets, like today, were specifically geared to serve optimally the markets of the "core" colonial powers. The surplus was invested in the "core" country and not in the "Third World."

6. Destroying local industry, forcing specialization in products, the prices of which could be easily manipulated to serve the Western market, strengthened markets fed by "Third World" capital. There was thus complete monopsony (one buyer who can set the price at which he buys) in the purchase from the "Third World" of its resources and complete monopoly (one seller who can set the price at which he sells) in the sale of colonial products to the "Third World'. (FieldHouse 1999 & Alexander 1996)

Consider the example of Nigeria. Nigeria produces one of the highest–grade oils in the world. This oil, bonnie light crude oil has great demand in the aviation and space programs in the developed world. However, the country including the people that live around the oil fields are plagued with unemployment, poverty and lack of health care (Chinyelu 1999).

Quantitative Findings:

Charles Glock and Rodney Stark (1967) reported empirical data that showed that Church members that held orthodox beliefs in the Bible were more likely to be anti–Semitic than less orthodox members (as quoted by Babbie 1992:82). In 1963 Lott and Lott provided empirical evidence that the "ethnocentrism" scale is related to the *"judgments about the relative superiority of one's own country as compared with another." (as quoted by Rosenberg 1968:17)*

Empirical evidence provides overwhelming evidence that nationalism and racism are both linked to "feelings about superiority." Empirical evidence also shows that orthodox Christianity is linked with racism. It is little surprise then that we find Christianity, racism (or white supremacy) and nationalism common features in the old "Apartheid" regime of South Africa, the West and the Ku Klux Klan[7]. The only thing that differs among them is the degree of openness about belief.

In searching for a proximate determinant of racism in the West, Christianity, as a factor precedes[8] other ideas about white supremacy. It has already been shown how it is correlated with such ideas. If a variable precedes another with which it is correlated, *"direction of determination"* can be demonstrated. Thus, using the criteria of causality in social sciences, elite sponsored Christianity can be termed as a "cause" of racism, or being related to it through some factor of causation (according to Mills' method of concomitant variation).

Martin Bernal writing about the roots of racism in the US stated:

The new racists tried to enlist religious backing for their ideological requirements. There was an emphasis among Christians of the 17th century for the Talmudic interpretation of the (creation) story of Genesis...in which it was Ham the ancestor of the Africans and not Ham's son Canaan who had been cursed by his father Noah and that that curse had consisted of blackness, ugliness and the fate of perpetual slavery (Ed. Vanhorne 1997: 83)

If we analyze data around the world and within white "settler" societies, it provides overwhelming evidence of how this interpretation of the 'pre-

---

[7] Alexander (1996) notes that the ideology of 'Apartheid' in South Africa was, "rich with references to Christianity, and divine destiny...and a common belief about 'white supremacy"(Alexander 1996:233).

[8] According to Griffin (1999), Kenneth Stamp noted that in the early seventeenth century in Virginia, "Blacks and whites seemed to be remarkably unconcerned about their physical differences. They toiled together in the fields, fraternized during leisure hours and, in and out of wedlock, collaborated in siring a numerous progeny." (As quoted by Griffin 1999: 26).

diction' of the Biblical curse has been self–fulfilled by being 'forced' upon African societies, around the globe.

An analysis of census data in the United States shows that the structure of the African American population in the United States resembles populations of the "Third–World" more closely than the general population of the society in which they reside. The African American population is younger than the white population having a median age of 30 years compared to 38.1 for whites. Similarly "Third World" populations are consistently younger than the developed world because of higher fertility and mortality. Only 8% of African Americans are over 65 compared to 14% of whites. Life expectancy for black males is 67, while that of white males is 74. Similarly life expectancy in the developed world is consistently higher (in some cases by over 30 years) than in the "Third World".

Infant mortality for white Americans is 6.0 per 1000 live births while that for blacks is 14.3 per 1000. The Median family income for white Americans is $46737 while that for black Americans is $29404. The median personal incomes are $14892 for black males (15 and over), and $24122 for white males (15 and over).

In the 1940s, blacks made up less than 10% of US population, yet 60% of prisoners executed were black. Unemployment rate for blacks (16 and above) is 11.3% while national unemployment rates have been around 3% nationally during Clinton's presidency. Of all people 25 to 34 years of age, 14.6% of blacks compared to 29% of whites had a bachelor degree. Private schools in the United States are almost entirely white. Fifty percent of all private schools had black enrollment of less than 9%, even though almost half of the private school students came from central cities, where minorities aren't even minorities (Ed. Wright. 2001). Murder victims are disproportionately black males. Fifty black males per 100,000 population were murdered in 1995 compared to 7 white males per 100,000. Black males make less money than white males in similar occupational positions, which require similar levels of skill. The median income of white males with a bachelor's degree is $43,335, that of a black male with a similar degree is $33,217. Fifteen percent of black males in the black labor force are managers compared to 30% of whites in the white labor force. However, 32% of blacks are laborers compared to only 18% of whites.

Environmental racism is witnessed clearly in the southern United States. Out of the 27 landfills operating in 48 states, a third are located in five southern states. The total capacity of these represents 60% of the nation's total landfill capacity. Blacks make up 20% of the south's population, yet zip codes of minority areas represent over 63% of the total landfill capacity of the south (Bullard 2000:33).

Economic exploitation and detachment from the mainstream society, leads to a profile of African Americans that closely resembles the profile of "Third World" countries. Distribution of diseases also reveals the colonial status of African Americans in the US. African Americans and Hispanics make up around 15% of the US population yet they make up 49% and 20% of all AIDS cases reported among those 13 to 19 (*www.icare.to/caucus/health*). Black women are three times more likely to die while pregnant and four times more likely to die at childbirth than white women are. The mortality stratum for all Africans (Child/adult) is either high or very high while that for all Europeans is low to very low. Only the Russian republics and some countries in the former Eastern European Soviet block have high adult mortality among Europeans.

The American Indian death rate from diabetes is 380% higher than that for the White population (27.8 per 100, 000 compared to 7.3 for Whites). Whites are three times more likely to undergo bypass surgery than non–Whites, improving their probability of survival. Similarly poor urban Black and Hispanic neighborhoods have an average of 24 physicians per 100, 000 people compared to 69 per 100,000 in poor White communities.

The introduction of disease by white settlers that devastated the indigenous population is well documented in history. From the 1770s, venereal disease was introduced among the Maori in New Zealand. In the 1790s influenza and TB entered the population. This devastated the indigenous community, which had no resistance against such "foreign" diseases. Beginning in 1769 when Captain James Cook entered New Zealand, the Maori outnumbered the settlers 40 to 1. By the 1870s the demographic picture of the Maori changed. The settlers outnumbered them 6 to 1. In the 1880s only 30% of Maori girls reached their 30th birthday (Ed.Stasiulis 1995:42).

Stasius and Japphan write about disease and the American Indians:

More devastating to the American Indians than changes wrought by trade were the scourges of disease against which Native peoples had little or no immunity (small pox, influenza, bubonic plague, yellow fever and so on), and the intrusion of Christian missionaries. It is now estimated that 20 waves of pestilence killed as much as 90% of the original population..(Ed Stasiulis 1995:102)

Indigenous people within the so–called white 'settler' societies like Canada, Australia, New Zealand and the United States have suffered fates similar to or worse than the creation of the "Third World". For example modern estimates place the pre–Columbus population of North America at 10 to 12 million. By the 1890s, it was reduced to about 300, 000. In Australia, Native/Aboriginal children of mixed–race were forcibly removed from their parent's home and given to adoptive white families as a form of "polite" genocide. They thus grew up without knowledge of their roots, being termed the "Stolen Generation".

The "Stolen Generation" inquiry found that:

"From about 1946, laws and practices which, for the purpose of eliminating indigenous cultures, promoted the removal of indigenous children for rearing in non–indigenous institutions and households were in breach of the international prohibition of genocide (Commission on Human Rights, 56th session).

Consider this 'testimony', by the Indians (based upon the reality of their experience) who seized Alcatraz Island in the San Francisco Bay area in 1969:

> *We feel that this so called Alcatraz Island is more than suitable for an Indian Reservation as determined by the white man's own standards. By this we mean that this place resembles most Indian reservations in that:*

1. *It is isolated from modern facilities.*

2. *It has no fresh running water.*

3. *It has inadequate sanitation facilities.*

4. *There are no oil or mineral rights.*

5. *There is no industry, so unemployment is very great.*

6. *There are no health care facilities.*

7. *The soil is rock and non–productive, and the land doesn't support game.*

8. *There are no educational facilities*

9. *The population has always exceeded the land base.*

10. *The population has always been held as prisoners and kept dependant upon others.*

> *Further it would be fitting and symbolic that ships from all over the world, entering the Golden Gate, would first see Indian land, and thus be reminded of the true history of this nation…"(Luhamn & Gilman 1980:189)*

Consider the case of Canada. According to some estimates, the unemployment rates for the Native American population in Canada has never gone below 80%, and most of those working are working at projects funded by the government (Powless 1985). In 1970, 24% of Indian males made more than $6000 per year compared to 52% of Canadian males. The earnings of the average Canadian are 29% higher than those of the Native Indian man. The proportion of Canadian men in professional and technical positions is nearly twice as high as those in the Indian labor force (18% compared to 8.6%). The average Canadian man earns 35% more than the average native man in the same occupation with the same skill level. In 1969, 80% of the Indian families were below the poverty line. The death rate for Indian people is six times that national average and the infant mortality rates are more than twice the national average. The life expectancy at one year of age is 63.4 years for Indians and 72.8 for the general population. Suicide among Indians is six times the national average and violent deaths are four to five times the national average. In 1974, 54% of the Indian population was using social assistance compared to 6% of the non–Indian population. The juvenile delinquency rate for natives is three times that of the national average. In 1979 Native people represented 1.3 percent of the Canadian population yet they were 9.3% of the penitentiary population.

In his report *Native People and Employment: A National Tragedy (1985)*, Richard Powless concludes:

> *The greatest and single most cogent reason for the current situation of Native people in Canada has been this inability to understand and accept the value and legitimacy of other peoples and cultures in Canada. In essence this is racism. Canada's history and system of governance and behavior have institutionalized this racism into current reality (Powless 1985:5)*

Australia is another example. Just as the patterned appearance of the ghetto in the inner cities of the United States, the appearance of affluence in close proximity to poverty is found in this 'white' settler state. The life expectancy of indigenous people in Australia is 20 years less than that of the non–indigenous population. Similarly indigenous people account for 31% of all Australians who live in abandoned dwellings or are "homeless" by all real measures. The unemployment rate for the indigenous population is twice that for the non–indigenous white population.

Compare the above data to an almost similar pattern of disparity (Table 1) found among the white 'settler' states and the former colonized non–white world. Global poverty is the rule and not the exception. Wages in third–world countries are 80 to 90 percent lower than in the West. Fifteen percent of the world's population (the rich countries of the West) controls over 80 percent of total world income (Chossudovsky 1997:35). Given that roughly 30 percent of the population in those countries controls over 50 percent of their resources, an even smaller group controls the world (Blau 1999:5). Over 85 percent of the world population get less than 20 percent of total world income. The poorest 20% of the world's population get around 1% of world income (Macionis 1996:189).

The numbers however, are only partially telling. They understate and mask true picture of global poverty, as their provision is based on a relative assessment of poverty. For example, according to the World Bank, the 'upper–poverty' line is defined as a per capita income of $1 a day. Those that earn more than $1 a day are defined as non–poor by such a definition. Thus poverty is grossly understated. Compare this to the U.S with a per–capita income of over $20,000 a year, one in five is defined as poor (Chossudovsky 1997:43).

According to Marxian analysis of stratification, economic oppression of minorities in capitalism is necessary. Racism thus becomes a screen, which the capitalist elite uses in order to pit groups of people against each other. If people can be distinguished easily and social consciousness can be molded by use of religion etc, to convince a group of people that 'others' are inferior to them, the emphasis of conflict shifts from its source, the capitalists, to the masses.

TABLE 1

REGION	LIFE EXPECTANCY (YEARS)	INFANT MORTALITY RATE Per 1000 live births	GNI. PPP PER CAPITAL IN US $	POPULATION DENSITY PER SQ MILE	POPULATION INCREASE 2001 TO 2050 PERCENT	TOTAL FERTILITY RATE
Western Africa (AVERAGE)	51	88	1000	101	393%	5.8
Eastern Africa (AVERAGE)	50	97	850	102	128%	5.7
Middle Africa (AVERAGE)	48	113	1500	39	203%	6.6
South Asia (AVERAGE)	61	72	2250	362	66%	3.4
United States	77	7.1	25440	77	45%	2.1
Canada	79	5.5	31910	8	18%	1.4
Australia	79	5.7	23850	6	29%	1.7

US Bureau of Census 1995 & Population Reference Bureau, 2001 Washington, DC

Oppression of the minorities serves a dual purpose, being profitable in addition to being a screen. Minorities can be hired for low wages to do the work no one else wants to do. This not only reinforces the stereotype that they are 'inferior' and easily exploited, it provides so called 'empirical' evidence in favor of the 'ideology of superiority' based upon the theoretical construct of Social Darwinism. The real cause, the institutional arrangement of the elite, is thus masked. It is not only the *interpretation* of religion but also the *interpretation* of 'science', pseudo–science, that becomes the 'opium of the masses'. As a result stereotypes emerge that are perpetuated by incomplete information and casual/subjective empirical observation that ignores the context of the situation. Stereotypes thus become a cost–effective "weapon of oppression", employed by the elite for maximum profitability and resource allocation.

Evaluating a list of eight Black stereotypes including "prefer to accept welfare" and have "less native intelligence", 75% of the Whites agreed with one or more and over 50% agreed with two or more, in a recent national survey of the Anti–Defamation League. About 30% or more agreed with four or more. In a 1994 National Opinion Research Center (NORC) survey about the work orientation of Blacks, only 16% listed Blacks as hardworking. Whereas only 7% placed Whites on the "lazy" end of the spectrum, a little under 50% placed Blacks in that category (Feagan–White Racism).

Racialized emotions are an effective way to ensure de facto, that old laws of separation are respected even when they have been made illegal on the books. In a 1990, two–thirds of the Whites said that they would have a negative reaction if a close relative married a Black person. Only 5% said that they would have a positive reaction (Feagan–White Racism).

Neocolonization & Perpetuation of Poverty:

W.E.B Dubois, sums up the cumulative effects of slavery on the economic life of African Americans after emancipation (what happened in the "Third World" was an exact parallel in many ways):

"I will not stop to ask whose duty it was, but I insist it was the duty of someone to see that these working men were not left alone and unguided, without capital, without land, without skill, without economic organization, without even the bald protection of law, order and decency,–left in a great land not to settle down to slow and careful internal development, but destined to be thrown almost immediately…in an economic system where every participant is fighting for himself, and too often *utterly regardless* of the rights or welfare of his neighbor (Dubois 1903:192)."

A modern political scientist, Clarence Stone writes:

> *"A brutally suppressed community overtime is conditioned to coping with disappointment and frustration. Thus they lose the motivation to develop (Stone 1993:15,1,21)."*

In 1881, Cecil Rhodes (using wealth from African Gold and Diamonds) formed a secret society to create a federation of all English–speaking people. This federation became the foundation on which the Council on Foreign Relations (CFR) in America and Royal Institute for International Affairs in Britain were founded. They comprise of the economic and political elite who shape "consistent" Western policy all over the world and who helped create the League of Nations, British Commonwealth, United Nations, Treaty of Rome, NATO and the G–7 (Alexander 1996:206). It is no surprise then that all these organizations have failed to realize world equity.

> *"There is no good in much of their **secret conferences** except in them that enjoin charity for goodness and reconciliation among humankind…(Koran 4:114)"*

Plans for the perpetuation of poverty were already underway during World War II. In 1944 Britain and the United States met at a conference at Bretton Woods, in the State of New Hampshire. This conference would ensure the subjugation and poverty of the 'Third World' till the present day and well into the future.

It was realized that it was no longer in the best interest of the West to maintain formal colonies. It would be more cost–effective to "in formalize" the control and ensure the integration of 'resource–supplying' countries into the capitalist economy, implicitly based on 'separate–development'–(similar to apartheid in South African or 'Jim Crow' in America). Thus were born the International Monetary Fund (IMF) and the International Bank for

Reconstruction and Development (later a part of the World Bank) (Danaher 1994:1).

The implicit agenda was the continuation of colonization without formal colonies while the explicit agenda was the treatment of 'Third–World economic pathologies' by providing 'economic medicine' (Chossudovsky 1997:33). The 'economic pathologies' of the "Third World" nations include over–valued currencies, high public expenditure, low taxes, low interest rates etc. What are termed 'Third World' pathologies are surprisingly enough 'positive' campaign issues for the Western economy. Thus we hear presidential candidates advocating lower taxes, higher spending on education and health and economic growth without inflation. If their domestic agenda were what the IMF is offering as "solution" to the "Third World", we would probably see an unstable government, riots and a not so exemplary "democracy".

This same cultural elite also discusses the life–style 'pathology' of the 'underclass' in America. The pathologies in the 'underclass' are normally described as laziness or lack of work ethic, drug addiction, alcohol abuse, an easy attitude towards sex and a lack of commitment to marital stability (Hadjor 1995:114). However if such were the pathologies of the 'underclass' then the 'over class' especially the Hollywood elite and role models of society suffer from the same illness. Nobody however, discusses what 'medicine' to give to them.

The conservative right in America argues that the ghetto dwellers have bad "work–ethic". "Why don't they go out of the ghetto and travel to where the jobs are," they say. They however conveniently forget historical facts. African Americans did travel long distances to seek employment in the North after the cotton industry started using labor saving devices in the South. Why "travelling" to the suburbs is not done to seek jobs that moved out of the cities, has to do with something other than distance. A similar "culture of poverty" style argument has been used to show the 'benefits' of colonization that European colonizers provided to an "ailing" culture in Asia and Africa.

Advocates of colonization similarly argued that the 'whole' of Africa lacked the work ethic. Setting up industries in Africa would thus have not worked, they said. 'People did not like travelling long distances to work,' they say (Fieldhouse 1999). However, these arguments are naïve to the fact that the "same" people whom they say wouldn't travel, do travel long distances to overcrowd "mega–cities" in the 'Third World' in search for employment. The 'mega–city' phenomenon has almost become an ecological pattern in most of the poorer countries of Asia and Africa. For the majority of these people, it is a first time trip from a rural to urban area, for the explicit purpose of employment, without any coercion like a 'hut' or 'head' tax of the colonial era.

The only change that the colonial powers brought about through such coercion was speeding up, without corresponding development, a surplus labor force to meet its profit and political agenda throughout the world. The forced migration of this 'surplus' whenever and wherever the metropolis desired is ample proof of this assertion. In many ways these coercive measures helped develop a worsening work ethic (rather than a positive one) as they interfered with people's freedom and creativity by making them mere mechanical operators (and extensions of machines), at below subsistence level wages, with little or no choice of investing their surplus in their own growth and development. The problem of the 'discouraged worker' has been clearly demonstrated in economic literature. In most cases, the local workers in Asia and Africa were paid ten times below what Europeans doing the same work were paid. Further, the pay was so menial that it could not even support the person, who then had to grow food to survive (Rodney 1982:149).

Another common tactic employed by the oppressor on the oppressed, to show 'sincerity' is to employ people of the oppressed group in such institutions. The World Bank and the IMF employs a large number of people from the 'Third World' in relatively senior positions. As a result we find Vice Presidents of different sections of the Bank with names like Masood, Ibraheem, or Ismail. Colonial England employed a similar tactic in the colonies. In order to get predatory information about the masses; Britain employed indigenous elements 'below' the European ruling elite. These officials began the never–ending cycle of 'Third World' political corruption (Fieldhouse 1999:79). Similar instances can be found today in police organizations in the United States, set up to control the ghetto and prevent race riots. Race riots erupted in the United States in 1964, in nine separate cities in 1965, to a total of 128 cities in 1967. The Kerner Commission report proposed that to keep race riots in check, apart from Aid for black businesses, more black troops should be hired to give "insight" into problems "before they occurred." (Hadjor 1995:175). Thus were appointed African American police chiefs who brutally cracked down on black communities.

Sociologist Philip Selznick, described this process of co–optation:

> *"One means of winning consent is to co–opt elements into the leadership or organization, usually elements which in some way reflect the sentiment, or possess the confidence of the relevant public or mass…It is met in colonial countries, where the organs of alien control reaffirm their legitimacy by co–opting native leaders into the colonial administration. We find it in the phenomena of "crisis patriotism" where formally disfranchised groups are temporarily given representation in the councils of government in order to win their solidarity in a time of national stress (American Sociological Review 13:1948:25–35, as quoted by Shafirtz & Ott)."*

In 1955 the General Agreement on Tariffs and Trade (GATT) was ratified leading eventually to the development of the World Trade Organization (WTO) in 1995. The benefits of these organizations for the most part have accrued to international banks and transnational corporations. They imply a "supervision" of 'Third World' countries. The conditionalities of the WTO have given a new 'legal' setting to the relationship between the West and the 'Third World'. The elite in the 'Third World' countries that accept funds from the agencies mentioned above agree to 'sell' their sovereignty, by accepting conditions for economic restructuring and policing to ensure compliance by the West (Chossudovsky 1997:35). Debtor nations have to give up their control of fiscal and monetary policy and Western institutions dictate their financial budgets and the working of their Central Bank. Thus every debtor country has a nominal government having even less power than subject local governments of the colonial era.

'Democratic' Loans: One of the first big loans that the World Bank made was on August 7, 1947. It was given for reconstruction to the colonialist government of the Netherlands. The Dutch had just sent 145000 troops to crush the anti–colonialist uprising in the East Indies. In 1966 the Bank, in defiance of the United Nations, continued to lend money to Portugal [and its colonial domination of Angola and Mozambique) and South Africa (and its apartheid). At this time in history the Bank was not profitable and had few lenders in outside regimes fighting wars. This however was to change in the late 1960 and early 1970s.

Loaning Out Poverty: The boom in the oil prices in 1973 and the US recession forced the loaning of money to the 'Third World' at close to zero (sometimes negative) interest rates. This money was used to purchase U.S and Western imports, resulting in economic growth in the West and the creation of over 2 million jobs (Alexander 1996:114). Just like a modern day credit–card company that makes borrowing attractive by a short period of low interest lending, at the end of which the rate jumps to unreasonable levels, the U.S suddenly increased interest rates in 1979.

The total outstanding debt of developing countries was $62 billion in 1970; increased to $481 billion in 1980 and in 1996 stood at over $2 trillion (Chossudovsky 1997:46). By the middle of the 1980s, the poor countries of the world were giving more in debt servicing to the rich West than was being received in the form of all inputs (loans, foreign investments and aid).

Banks and institutions that set up shop in poor minority communities in the United States, similarly drain the community of their resources.

The same system is at play with its predictable pattern of winners and los-
ers. Chinyelu presents a case study of the Freedom National Bank that was
established in 1964 in Brooklyn to serve as a community institution for
providing loans to African Americans for home purchase and small business establishment:

> *Freedom National collected $50 million in deposits from their
> two Brooklyn branches, yet woefully made only three mortgage
> loans, totaling a mere $130,000 to Brooklynites seeking to pur-
> chase homes...In other instances, members of the bank's manage-
> ment board pushed through unsecured loans, either for themselves
> or for their friends, some of which were not repaid (Chinyelu
> 1999:84–85)*

The loans that were given by the bank and the IMF came with strict
conditions. They were 'policy–based'. In the beginning of the 1970s, the
Peterson Report in the United States recommended to ' establish a frame-
work of principles, procedures and institutions, that will ensure the effective use of assistance funds and *the achievement of US national interests*
(McNeill 1981:52)[9]. The 'weighted' vote of the United States and the
West in decisions is comfortably placed in such institutions, to guarantee
decisions in their favor.

Consumers know that credit–card companies are happy if you make
the minimum payments on your credit cards, thereby maximizing the
profits of their company via interest and 'late–fees'. Now imagine if they
had the liberty to "force" you to use the convenience checks that they mail

---

[9] The IMF classifies countries in terms of "resource usefulness" to the West. In terms of
murder and rape, the countries of the West are the 'least developed', however that is not
the criteria that the West has dictated (Alexander 1996:80). From 1982 to 1990 the total
amount of money transferred from the "Third World" to the West was around six times
the amount of the Marshall Plan that helped rebuild Europe after World War II. How
come the "Third World" isn't six times or even equally developed? (Alexander 1996)

you, and also dictate where you do the spending–this is a close approximation to how the World Bank and IMF operate with 'Third World' countries. If your debt becomes unmanageable, you have to work to pay off the debt, whether you like your current job or not, otherwise you risk falling through the security net.

The IMF and the World Bank have devised a way to be even more profitable than the credit card companies. They don't require the poor countries to pay back the principal (at the moment) as they realize that most of them cannot, even if they wanted to, so they just require the periodic payment of the interest on the loans. This is called 'debt–servicing' by 'rescheduling' debt payments.

However, apart from being extremely profitable, resulting in a net flow of capital from the 'Third World' to the West (poor people feeding the rich), it gives the rich industrial countries of the West complete control over the national economic policies of these countries. There are tight conditionalities to these loans, and deadlines to their implementation in the debtor's economy. The changes that these institutions require are not based on the implementation of an investment program or project; they are "policy" changes that affect the entire economy and especially the majority population in these countries, those that are the most deprived. The names and terms of the loans explicitly suggest the objectives. They are called "structural adjustment loans (SAL)," or "Sector adjustment loans." The IMF calls part of its loaning facilities "Systematic Transformation Facility (STF)".

On paper, the loans are contingent upon Macro–economic stabilization and structural reforms. By Macro stabilization, the IMF–World Bank requires a country to devalue its currency, liberalize its prices and snip and cut the country's budget, called austerity measures. This is required of countries whose GNP is less than General Motors or the Ford Motor Company. Fifteen percent of the world's population living in the Western industrial countries are responsible for nearly 80 percent of world expenditure (UN Human Development Report 1998). Yet the same people, who spend the most, want to promote "austerity" in the 'Third World'. These "Ghetto Lords" enforce the following:

i) Currency devaluation: This is almost universal in the IMF–World Bank policy agenda. A devalued currency almost overnight sends the 'Third World' economy in question into a price hike. Imports become more expensive while exports of the country become cheaper to the West, through the reduction of the dollar price of labor cost. The extra dollars that the government earns or saves are supposed to be used for debt servicing i.e. recycled back to the West. The effect of devaluation is that the domestic price of food and medicine and public services–common necessities–goes up almost overnight. Thus the poor are made poorer. Those who have saved all their lives, lose the real value of their money in a matter of hours. However, commodities and raw materials required by the rich countries of the West become cheap to them but expensive for 'Third World' home consumption and lead to a booming economy in the West with a 2.2 percent inflation rate, compared to the double digit inflation in the 'Third World'.

After adopting the 1991 IMF plan, the price of rice in India rose 50 percent in six months and the real–earnings of the textile industries fell by 60 percent due to inflation. This directly affected the lives of over 60 million people. Adding to the misery were the reduced wages of rice–paddy workers, around $0.57 for a day's work. This amount, 0.57 cents, contrary to popular opinion, is not a fortune in India. Adjusted for cost of living (purchasing power parity) differences, it could buy only $2 worth of goods in America. A monthly salary of less than $50, if they were in the US (Alexander 1996:109). Can anyone survive on $2 a day in the United States? However, the Indian government didn't care because most of these "low–wage" workers were of the "untouchable" class. At best they needed "controlling" and "austerity" similar to the view of the West towards the 'Third World'.

After the flood in Bangladesh in 1991, which killed over 140,000 people, the IMF enforced its devaluation program. The retail price of rice went up by over 50 percent causing a famine and killing tens of thousands of people (on paper that is). The real number was much higher, as the emergency food, being appropriated by indigenous officials never reached the starving masses (UN Human Development Report 1998).

ii) Anti–inflationary program: However, after causing inflation via devaluation, the IMF wants the government to enact an "anti–inflationary program".

The IMF method of attacking inflation is to cut demand and put a tight control on the money supply. However, devaluation, which was the real cause of inflation, is ignored. Contraction of demand implies that public expenditure is to be controlled. The only way government expenditure can be controlled is to lay off public employees or to cut social service programs. This has a double effect. It cuts government spending as well as private consumption spending. If people don't have jobs they spend less on consumption. Therefore, money is freed to service the debt while people live at near starvation levels. Global consumption expenditure has grown at an average of 3 percent since 1970, however in the poorest of the 'Third World' countries it has fallen dramatically. Both public and private consumption per capita in Africa has fallen over 20% since 1980.

Another way expenditure can be controlled is to cut investment and infrastructure building. Thus projects like public utilities and water are stopped midway. Bubonic plague in India in 1994 was directly attributed to the "IMF structural reform program of 1991" which cut spending in that sector. Out of 4.4 billion people in developing countries, 60 percent lack access to sanitation and nearly forty percent have no access to clean water and a quarter have no housing (UN Human Development Report 1998). About 17 million die of curable infectious/parasitic diseases like Malaria and Diarrhea etc. Yet the "noble" dream of the World Bank, according to their web site, is "a world free of poverty."

There is yet another way that demand can be reduced and that is to reduce foreign imports. However, the IMF–World Bank agenda strictly forbids any control on trade. Not only this, imports from the West are forcibly encouraged by "quick disbursing policy–based loans (Chossudovsky 1997:53)" for importing consumer goods and food from rich countries. Not only is the debt enlarged, it earns extra profit for the West as more of the devalued currency has to be used to pay for the "same" amount of imports.

The devaluation discussed above causes a short–term boost to the 'Third World' economy by increasing exports. The West's control of the governing bodies of 'Third World' nations ensures that the profit from this, what is left after debt servicing, goes to overseas bank accounts, in the West (by making the free movement of foreign exchange one of the conditionalities of loan provision in many countries). The short–term boost however is over soon. Devaluation by the other 'Third World' countries, all fighting for crumbs from the "master's table" soon restore the balance of trade to the former level, leaving the country poorer and the misery greatly magnified. This sets a viscous cycle of misery with riots, government overthrows, and near–war situations in many of these countries.

iii) Separation of Central Bank from politics: One of the conditions of the IMF is that the debtor nation separates the Central Bank from all political power. Thus the IMF and not the government of the country control the money supply and money creation. Therefore the economic development or non–development is now directly in the hands of the 'foreign' power, the IMF and the World Bank, with its decision vote in the hands of the United States and its Western European allies. The influence is such that the heads of many of the Central Banks are former senior officials of the International Financial Institutions (IFI), and sometimes receive salary supplements from these creditors (Chossudovsky 1997:58).

iv) Public Expenditure Review: The IMF–World Bank monitors all public expenditure by the government through its "Public Expenditure Review (PER)". It has required that certain 'vulnerable' groups be targeted but overall the state reduces its expenditure on such things like health and education. During the 1980s, spending on education in African IMF countries fell by 25% according to the UN Commission on Africa (Alexander 1996:127).

The reduction of expenses on social services, which were small to begin with, is not a one–time demand by the IMF and the World Bank. They require a "moving target" approach. Once the target is reached, a further reduced target is set for the next period, causing a further cutback in public spending. At the same time, spending on the military industry, especially where the sellers are the western firms is never discouraged. The major part of the expenses of many of these nations is on arms import. In NATO countries, military spending fell by 33 percent between 1987 and 1996, however in South Asia, it increased by 13 percent and in some countries like Indonesia and Malaysia, by over 35 percent (UN Human Development Report 1998).

These arms were imported in the major part from the West. It is therefore expedient for the West to keep situations in these countries at a 'near war' level. The 'conflicts', that are kept alive in many of these countries have already been decided upon by the United Nations (Kashmir and Palestine is the case in point) but are deliberately ignored by Western powers that seek to benefit from the status quo. In keeping with this contradictory policy, certain other United Nations' resolutions are forcibly extracted and executed with lightening speed in the "Desert Storm" fashion.

In the 1970s Somalia was almost self–sufficient in food and Vietnam had a 90% literacy rate. After they allowed the West to implement "Structural Adjustment" in their economies, we saw that Somalia was starving and enrollment in Vietnamese schools dropped by over 25% in a short period (Chossudovsky 1997).

v) Investment in infrastructure: In controlling expenditure, 'ceilings' are placed on all expenditures of investments. The state cannot choose or employ its own public to build infrastructure. Though the "Public Investment Projects (PIP), the IMF–World Bank become brokers of all investment projects in the 'Third World' country. It is required that 'competitive bidding' among select international firms are the criteria.

International firms are employed which charge large amounts of money in management and consultation fees (intellectual property rights). A huge proportion of the debt is used for such "technical assistance." Thus once again, no capital is sent and a few numbers are added to the computer totals. The money changes hands in the same block of rich Western countries who compete for contracts to build. Locals are kept out of the planning process but local laborers do most of the building at marginal wages. Thus the external debt is enlarged, and local resources are not used for developing technical expertise but for basic "raw" labor, as against "planning science".

Another way the IMF–World Bank stunts domestic growth in the poor nation is by controlling the price of fuel and utilities. The price often inflated several hundred percent, forces many manufacturers into bankruptcy by fictitiously increasing the cost of manufacture and internal transportation. Thus imports from the West appear as the only alternative. The East India Company achieved a similar motive in colonial times when it imposed "internal–transit duties" on local manufactured goods, thus aborting a newly forming industry. The same is happening today in Sub–Saharan Africa where local farmers cannot transport their produce to urban areas for sale (Chossudovsky 1997:63).

Yet another way employed by the IMF–WB to reduce investment (in the domestic economy to keep it at a resource providing, non–manufacturing level) is the deregulation of domestic banking and the free entry of foreign banks in the market. The government is not allowed to give subsidized loans, and a strict control of money creation together with other economic requirements of the IMF–WB, drives up interest rates to unreal levels. It becomes impossible to borrow money to invest in industry as its 'opportunity cost' is too high. It would thus be more profitable to keep that money in interest–earning accounts. This encourages non–investment and an inflow of "black money (money that has escaped taxation)" and "dirty money (illegal trade)" into the 'Third World' money market.

The advantage of this is temporary for the domestic economy, which gets short–term relief in debt servicing. After a short gain there is a huge loss, as the elites in these countries, after laundering this money, send it to the West, whereas before it couldn't be sent as it was out of the system. Therefore, there is a double–exit of capital from the poor country. The exit that occurred when the funds were used for debt servicing and the exit that followed shortly thereafter in the form of laundered money sent to Western banks.

The IMF–WB policy encourages money laundering on a global level, where it suits the interest of the West. Where such laundering doesn't suit them (or is channeled back to the poor domestic economy), worldwide bank chains like the Bank of Credit and Commerce International (BCCI) are forcibly shut down, and their funds appropriated.

On a local scale, writing about the Freedom National Bank in Harlem, Chinyelu (2000) states:

> *"Earlier in 1990, when Freedom National was having problems, a much larger bank in Boston, The Bank of New England, was in a similar situation. However, the federal government made an effort to sustain the Bank of New England by depositing public funds in the Bank, while a the same time sharply cutting back similar deposits at the Freedom National Bank, thus hastening the collapse of this small minority owned institution. Equally disturbing was the Federal Deposit Insurance Corporation willingness to cover the Bank of New England's $3 Billion in uninsured deposits, while not willing at least initially to cover Freedom National's $8 to $10 million in uninsured deposits (Chinyelu 1999:85)."*

vi) Removal of Import Quotas: The policies that encourage Western imports at the detriment of the developing domestic industry is further strengthened by the insistence of the IMF–World Bank that import quotas and tariffs be reduced if not eliminated. This has two effects; i) It leads to an increase in luxury goods being imported into the domestic economy, thereby resulting in a further outflow of capital to the West from poor countries and ii) a reduction of custom duties to the domestic government which could have been spent on education, health and other public services. Most of all however, this "increase" in spending is not due to a good economy but is sustained on either "short–term" export gains by devaluation (discussed above) or on "adjustment loans" i.e. further debt (also discussed above).

vii) Privatization of Enterprises: Another policy advocated with a vengeance (by threat of cutting off funding) by the IMF–World Bank is the privatization of state owned enterprises. In the best scenario for the West, the most profitable 'Third World' ventures are bought in exchange for debt servicing by Western firms. In this regard, Citibank has been doing a lot of shopping overseas. In most cases these transactions are just "on–the–book". There is no transfer of capital to the poor country. The "debt" number is reduced by a small amount on a computer "in" the West and ownership of a key industrial player in the 'Third World' is transferred to Western ownership. The profits from this venture are now, instead of being invested in the domestic country, being sent to the West (in the case of Citibank, to the US). The poor country has gained nothing in the process. Since the mid 1960s history has shown that the debt number that went down slightly in that computer "in" the West has gone up more than 3200 percent, as poor countries got buried in "forced" debt.

Another privatization venture enforced by the IMF is the privatization of land by issuing land titles to farmers. The income so generated would help the debtor country pay off the interest on the loans taken from IFI's through the IMF–WB. However, this displaces traditional farmers, many of whom find themselves without land to grow food, almost overnight.

viii) Domestic Tax reforms: These have been the agenda of the IMF–World Bank as well. They have insisted that a domestic sales tax be applied on 'common necessities'. The burden of this tax invariably falls on the lower and middle class consumers who are already under the burden of reduced real wages and inflation (caused by IMF devaluation). The contradictory nature of this policy is revealed when these agencies insist that "tax breaks and tax holidays" be given to foreign investors. Those investors who will cause a slight reduction in a computer number and will send most of the domestic growth abroad.

Not only has empirical evidence shown the disasters caused by the IMF–World Bank on an almost universal scale, especially in Africa and Asia, the IMF and World Bank have acknowledged their failures, without a change in policy, however:

> *"Although there have been a number of studies on the subject over the past decade...In fact it has often been found that the programs are associated with a rise in inflation and a fall in the growth rate (IMF Staff Papers 37:2:1990, p196, p222–as quoted by Chossudovsky 1997:69)."*

Conclusion & Solutions:

As we saw above, legislation based solutions are extremely limited in the results they can get given institutionalized racism, which I have argued is the cause for the continuing exploitation of the "Third World" by the West.

The clearest historical/empirical proof of this is the discriminatory treatment of non–white colonies compared to the white 'settler–states' like Australia, New Zealand, South Africa and Canada. In these countries, the White minority was allowed complete control over domestic resources and was free to invest the surplus in the local economy and protect their local industry from being devastated by forced–exchange.

The British invested in infrastructure in these 'settler' countries and money was loaned at rates that followed local banking rates, and thus were not unusually inflated or exploitive. Wholesale killing of the non–white indigenous populations by the white settlers also restored a favorable population–resource ratio in most of these countries. Since there was no forced production in these 'settler–states' and they were allowed protectionism and the freedom to choose their own economic policy (Fieldhouse 1999:19), the products they chose to specialize in were products similar to those in the West and thus were more profitable and less susceptible to price fluctuations (Fieldhouse 1999: 130–162). The fact is that Britain treated these "settler states" as an extension of Britain and not "alien" like its Asian and African colonies:

> *As its base, the white settler society construct refers to the intention of colonial administrators…an 'overseas extension' or replica of British society. Hence the dominant culture, values and institutions of the society mimic those of the 'mother' country…(Ed. Staliusis et al 1995:97).*

We similarly saw that after the 'emancipation' of African Americans after the Civil War, the ideology that justified racism to the Western mind, persisted and resulted in a condition for the group that was little different than the 'informal' colonization of the 'emancipated' colonies after independence. The ideology, as we saw, exists today with a change in terminology.

Recently, Harvard professor and 'poverty expert' William Julius Wilson suggested in, *The Bridge over the Racial Divide (2000)*, that a broad based coalition be formed that discusses both white and black poverty matters and is non–race based (to attract the white majority). On paper it looks like a noble cause but in reality it doesn't deal with the source of the problem. It is a dangerous idea as it delays the addressing of real problems and tactfully serves as a tool of the elite in maintaining the status quo.

The very assumption that a "non–race based" coalition is needed to motivate action implicitly recognizes that white America is indifferent to the plight of black America unless their own concerns are addressed, in such a coalition. The problems of the 'Third World' have never been solved by such seemingly 'broad based' coalitions. The United Nations, the IMF, the World Bank all have 'noble aims' on paper and are seemingly 'broad based', yet the problems and the poverty of the Third World has only increased through most of their history. Small problems were addressed but the 'broad' issues remained unsolved due to an exploitive racist ideology.

Conditions in the "Third World" that are perpetuated by the global capitalist system result in an oppositional "terrorism culture". Selective empirical evidence of injustice perpetuated by the West, to the followers of such an "oppositional" culture reinforce their "Robin Hood" standing. Similar conditions in the inner cities leads to an oppositional "code of the street" and perpetuates street crime. On a wider scale, capitalist alienation, drugs and alcohol do the same (Anderson 1999: 111). Elijah Anderson in his ethnographic study, *The Code of the Street* (1999) states:

> *The emergence of an underclass isolated in urban ghettos with high rates of joblessness can be traced to the interaction of race and prejudice, discrimination and the effects of the global economy. These factors have contributed to the profound social isolation and impoverishment of broad segments of the inner–city black population…In their social isolation an oppositional culture, a subset of which is the code of the street, has been allowed to emerge, grow and develop…A larger segment of people are now not simply isolated but even more profoundly alienated from the wider society and its institutions." (Anderson 1999:316)*

1. New ideology:

If a lasting, just solution to the continued subjugation and periodic genocide of a majority of humankind is to be found, we need a new ideology. An ideology that demonstrates, in theory and action, the "one community" of humankind[10]. Malcolm X witnessed such unity in Mecca during *Hajj*, the Muslim pilgrimage.

---

[10] In the 1990s, U.S cities had an average '*segregation index*' of 66.5%. This means that around 67% of blacks would have to move to make the neighborhood integrated [Massey & Denton 1996:222]. Christian churches are even more segregated than U.S cities [Griffin 1999].

By emphasizing the common, non–hierarchical origin of humankind, under one creator God (Koran 4:1), the Koran constructs a society where illogical ideas of superiority are not only considered ignorant, they are looked upon as a major source of evil in the world.

The psychologist, Erik Erkison stated that our cultures create, "pseudospecies", i.e. false categories of race and nation that destroy our sense of ourselves as one species thereby encouraging hostility and violence. This explains how "easy" it becomes for the West, to justify to its culture the systematic genocide of millions of "non–white" people (as quoted by Zinn 1990:40). Such a justification is not possible if ideology is based 'exclusively' on a constitution that says:

> "O humankind! Be careful of God who created you of a single essence…(Koran 4:1)"

> "O humankind! We have created you male and female and divided you into nations and tribes for identity. The best of you in God's sight is the one most (socially) aware (Koran49: 13)"

> "And of God's signs is the creation of the heavens and the earth, and **the differences in your colors and languages**. Indeed in this are signs for those who have knowledge (Koran 30:22)"

> "You (men and women) issue one from the other (Koran 3:195)"

> "Let not a nation deride a nation…(Koran 49:11)"

A common, equity based ideology is critical for generating a "broad based" collective identity that seeks *transformative* social justice. It is only under such an ideology that individual and collective "identity frames" can be brought into synchrony to reduce the potential for identity disputes (Stoecker 1995). Without a common *justice based* ideology, "narrow issue frames" would result in a movement that at best achieves small goals and either disintegrates or is co–opted by the elite before any meaningful social change. As a result, without a change in ideology, all calls for "broad based coalitions" like Wilson's **Bridge Over the Racial Divide (2000)** are bound to fail, like the IMF, UN and World Bank have failed in achieving "transformative change" in the world.

The history of every human conflict and resulting injustice can be traced to the "selfish desire" of groups leading to factionalism (Koran 6:65), based upon an ideology of superiority. Without ideological shifts, even the oppressed workers, when they get a chance, become oppressors as *Michels'Iron Law of Oligarchy* makes clear.

Capitalism is designed to keep people apart through competition and individualism. The elite, taking advantage of the system and the market mechanism generated by Capitalism, lock individuals in a race for survival, pitting one against the other. By reducing the worth of everything, including human relationships to their "money" value, Capitalistic ideology and a society projected by such an ideology produces the worst form of "bondage" possible. "Slavery" to material objects, in which the purpose of life becomes their acquisition. A "slavery" in which those who are enslaved don't even realize the depth of their bondage.

Malcolm X said, and herein lies the solution:

> *"The Western world's most learned diplomats have failed to solve this grave race problem. Her learned legal experts have failed. Her sociologists have failed. Her civic leaders have failed. Her fraternal leaders have failed. Since all of these have failed to solve this race problem, it is time for us to sit down and reason. I am certain that we will be forced to agree that it takes God Himself to solve this grave racial dilemma (Haley, 1973)."*

2. Access to the media and communication networks:

Formal controls alone do not change minds and attitudes. People discover over time that laws can be violated and avoided. Positive public relations, especially through the media can have an immense influence on people's views. Black communities, which are among the poorest in this country, have lacked access to the media and effective public relations.

Because of segregation, the majority of White Americans find out about Black Americans as well as the 'Third World' through the media controlled by the an elite who want to perpetuate and rationalize a culture of "superior–subordinate" relationships.

The media is a very powerful and effective tool. It has been effectively used by Israel to change the image common Americans have about Jews. By carefully portraying the Holocaust, they have monopolized world sympathy in their favor. Compare this to the much larger scale genocide of American Indians and Africans during the slave trade, which nobody hears about. So powerful is this persuasion via the media that it makes the world ignore the genocide of Palestinians by the once persecuted Jews.

3. "Odious" Loans:

Most of the loans given by the IMF–World Bank were 'odious' loans. They were given to regimes supported by the West that were in most cases non–democratic. The people in these countries were never asked if they wanted the extra debt. Hence, the default of these loans and the complete writing off of these loans is justifiable (Danaher 1994). Not only did the regimes to which these loans were given, removed from office for corruption in some cases, they sent huge amounts of the same loans back to the West in terms of personal accounts and business and managerial contracts (McNeill 1981:54).

Thus, the people of the "Third World" should collectively, following the example of Mexico, refuse to make any payments on the loans (principal and interest). On the contrary they should demand the "time adjusted compensation" from the West for the "rape" of "Third World" resources by the colonial powers and for the free use of labor, unfair compensation and capital drain from the "Third World" during the colonial era and after.

4. Investment Banks, Cartels and Counter Trade Embargoes:

Cartels to control the price of primary commodities should be set up, so that the West doesn't gain an unfair advantage by its economic "warfare" on the 'Third World'. The example of the 1970s where, the "Third World" could collectively impose a *defensive* economic embargo against the West should serve as a benchmark for the restoration of the balance of power in the world.

Third World poverty receives lesser attention in the West than a few cent rise in the domestic price of U.S gas, as was witnessed last summer. Unless the ideology of racism is replaced by a completely different, more humane ideology, the "Third World" should pursue "de–linking" from the Western economy, engaging the West only where it is beneficial to the masses of the "Third World." This implies exiting all "broad based" coalitions that serve the interests of the West.

Regional investment banks in the "Third World" that cover certain blocks of countries should be established. The granting of loans to private "domestic" entrepreneurs based on the monitoring of their performance in the local economy should be envisioned.

Import subsidizing industries should be developed with maximum investment and protection. Trade within the 'Third World" block should be encouraged as against Western imports. When these "infant" industries grow up, trade can be liberalized on equal, non–predatory terms with the whole world.

5. Investment in Education and Information Technology:

The "Third World" should make maximum investment in developing its media to control the media warfare by the West (media that is controlled by a few elite–groups with vested interests). The West's export of the culture of racism, under the false pretense of "freedom" should be intellectually challenged. Boards that deal specifically with media issues and the communications of ideas should counteract, and bring to public notice injustice done in the name of "democracy" and "freedom".

The West developed scientifically, in a major way, due to information freely shared by Muslim merchants and the Islamic civilization. Science, Accounting, Mathematics and Algebra (including the number system), the philosophy of the Greeks, all came to the West through Islam (Alexander 1996:7 etc). The colonials, by non transfer of industrial knowledge, and the West nowadays by non transfer of "equal" technology, plays a game of "technology warfare" backed by a philosophy that, "*an educated Negro (or "Third World") is a dangerous Negro (or "Third World)* (W.E.B Dubois 1903: 71). "Skill mismatch" is the outcome of planned alienation, backed by a racist ideology.

Knowledge is nobody's property. New information gets its foundation on older information. It is nobody's right to block one level when the earlier level was not "invented" by him or her. Thus all intellectual property rights are illegal in the most part. Loops around barriers to education can be found if properly searched. The "Third World" in this information age needs to locate these loopholes. "Persuasion resources" should be directed towards the intellectuals so that they can see the "right" and "wrong" in issues based on justice. Such members will be the lifeline of the majority world if it is to survive in an age where information and knowledge are used as weapons because of racist ideologies, themselves based on ignorance.

6. Population–Resource Ratio:

Most countries, especially the poorest in Asia and Africa have a very unfavorable population to resource ratio. The population boom, as understood by sociologists, is not based on "free–will" choices but on a host of deterministic factors. These factors, like the lack of education or adequate diet are the direct legacy of colonialization in the case of the "Third World" and slavery, and institutionalized oppression in the case of the African American "underclass". If the other problems are taken care of, population levels will overtime, automatically adjust as reflected by the Demographic Transition Theory.

Hopefully in the long run, we can all succeed together and in the "perfect–world" humanity can grow as one. If not, then history has shown that empires like the West, built and sustained upon human suffering, eventually crumble from within. Let us also hope that the masses in the West recognize this and change the agenda of the elite before the West "self–destructs" forcing history to repeat itself.

> *"Systems have passed away before you. Travel in the earth and see the nature of the consequence for the tyrants…(Koran 27:69)"*

Bibliography:

Abrahamson, Mark. *Urban Enclaves.* 1996. St. Martin Press.

Alexander, Titus. *Unravelling Global Apartheid. An Overview of World Politics.*1996. Cambridge, MA. Polity Press.

Babbie, Earl. *The Practice of Social Research.* 6th ed. 1992. Wadsworth Publishing Co. California.

Blau, Joel. *Illusions of Prosperity: America's Working Families in an age of Insecurity.* 1999. Oxford University Press. New York.

Bullard, Robert D. Dumping in Dixie.3rd ed. 2000. Westview Press. Oxford.

Chossudovsky, Michel. *The Globalization of Poverty.*1997. Zed Books Ltd. London.

Carlyle, Thomas. *On Heroes and Hero Worship, and the Heroic in History–1918–*The Hero as a Prophet. London.

Castells, Manuel. *The City and the Grassroots: A cross–cultural Theory of Urban Social Movements.* Berkeley. University of California Press. 1983 [Chapter 17 & 18].

Delavignette. Robert. *Christianity and Colonialism.* 1964. Hawthorne Book Publishers. New York.

Danaher, Kevin. *50 Years is Enough.* 1994. South End Press. Boston.

Dubois, W.E.B. *The Souls of Black Folk. First Published 1903.* Ed. 1995. Signet Classics, New York.

Fieldhouse, D.K. *The West and the Third World.* 1999.Blackwell Publishers.

Fraser, Steven. Editor. *The Bell Curve Wars.* 1994. Basic Books New York.

Gans, Herbert. *The War against the Poor.* 1995. New York. Basic Books.

Griffin, Paul R. *Seeds of Racism in the Soul of America.* 1999.The Pilgrim Press. Cleveland.

Hadjor, Kofi Buenor. *Another America.* 1995. South End Press. Boston.

Heineman, Kenneth. *God is a Conservative.*1998. New York University Press. New York.

Hancock, Graham. *The Lords of Poverty.* 1989. Atlantic Monthly Press. New York.

Haley, Alex & Malcolm X. *The Autobiography of Malcolm X.*

Koran: Translation from the Arabic.

Kilbourne, Jean. *Deadly Persuasion.* 1999. The Free Press. New York.

Chinyelu, Mamadou. *Harlem Ain't Nothin' But a Third World Country.* 1999. Mustard Seed Press. New York.

Macionis, John J. *Society: The Basics.* 3rd edition. Prentice Hall. NJ

McNeill, Desmond. *The Contradictions of Foreign Aid.* 1981. Croom Helm, London.

Massey, Douglas S & Denton, Nancy A. *American Apartheid: Segregation and Making of the Underclass.* 1996. Harvard University Press.

Shariftz, Jay M & Ott, Stephen J (ed). *Classics of Organization Theory* ,5th ed. 2001. Harcourt. New York.

Mills, C. Wright. *The Power Elite.* 1956

Rosenberg, Morris. 1968. *The Logic of Survey Analysis.* Basic Books Inc. New York.

Riley, John. *Abraham Lincoln and the Emancipation Proclamation.* [retrieved 10/10/'00–http://www.thehistorynet.com/NationalHistoryDay/2000/emancipation.htm]

Rodney, Walter. 1982. *How Europe Underdeveloped Africa.* Howard University Press, Washington, DC.

Smith, Tom. *The American Family.* GSS 1998, University of Chicago.

Stasiulis, Daiva and Nira Yuval Davis. Editors. 1995. *Unsettling Settler Societies: Articulations of Gender, Race, Ethnicity and Class.* Thousand Oaks, California.

Stone, Clarence. *Urban Regimes and the Capacity to Govern.* 1993. Journal of Urban Affairs

Schaefer, Robert T & Lamm Robert P. *Sociology.* 6th ed. New York. McGraw Hill Companies.

Stoeker, Randy. 1995. *Community, Movement, Organization: The Problem of Identity Convergence in Collective Action. Sociological Quarterly.*

Takaki, Ronald T. *Reflections on Racial Patterns in America.* 1982. Ethnicity and Public Policy, University of Wisconsin (Pp.1–23).

Van Horne, Winston. Editor. *Global Convulsions: Race, Ethnicity and Nationalism at the End of the Twentieth Century.* 1997. State University of New York Press. New York.

2

Jihad & Media Terrorism

The media in our society, controlled by people having vested interests, fuels the misinformation and misconception concerning Jihad. As a result, a prejudiced attitude is so nurtured that whenever any terrorism takes place, the ones to blame are Muslims. The truth of this statement was demonstrated in the Oklahoma City Bombing incident of late April 1995. The damage so done by such cowardly acts of literary terrorism by the media, surpass national boundaries and create a culture of hate.

This chapter is divided into three sections: i) Jihad and Islamic warfare, ii) Islam in history and iii) Peace in Islam

I) Jihad and Islamic Warfare:

The word *Jihad* translated into English does not mean "Holy War" as people in the media ignorantly state. In the text of the whole Koran, the word "Holy War" cannot be found. The word Jihad in Arabic means, "struggle".

Jihad as the Koran makes clear, is a struggle in the way of God with oneself, and one's possessions. Islam only allows war as a defense . In the case of war, the attack is only to be directed against those who are fighting you. If the enemy kills your civilians, even then you are not supposed to kill their civilians till you are sure that those "civilians" are fighting against you to similarly kill you.

> *"Fight in the way of God against those who fight against you, but begin not hostilities. Indeed God does not love transgressors (Koran 2:192–193)."*

If the people you are fighting ask for peace, the Koran states that Muslims have an obligation to accept the peace and fight no more:

> *"..So if they hold aloof from you and wage not war against you and offer you peace. God allows you no way against them (Koran 4:90)."*

The Koran is very lenient even towards prisoners of war (i.e. those who are fighting against you who get captured):

> *"And if any of the idolaters seeks of you protection, grant him (her) protection till he hears the words of God, then convey him to his place of security. That is because they are a folk who know not..(Koran 9:6–8)."*

The Koran states that sometimes war is a necessity and has to be fought to check tyranny:

> *"How is it with you that you do not fight in God's way, when the feeble among the men, women and children are saying, "Our lord, bring us forth from this place whose people are tyrants. O God give us from your presence some protector and helper.'(Koran 4:75–76)."*

> *"..If God had not repelled some people by means of others, the earth would have been corrupted (Koran 2:251)."*

Sometimes, war is a necessity, for the cause of justice and to remove oppression, and as such it is very good and noble:

> *"Warfare is ordained for you though it is hateful for you. Yet it may happen that you will hate a thing even though it is good for you and love a thing that is bad for you. God knows, you don't know (Koran 2:216)."*

ii) Islam in History

The west has generally nourished the idea that Islam spread at the point of the sword. This reasoning led to the prejudice of Islam and terrorism taking root in Western society throughout Europe and America because of the acts of a few misled, ill informed, and uneducated people who are labeled "Muslims". The Taliban would be the case in point. This idea, historically nurtured deliberately by the elite in the West, to perpetuate hate among the masses, and fictitiously imposed upon Islam, was adopted by segments of the Islamic world that were gullible because of a lack of education. This label (of "Militant Islam" or the oft–repeated label "Islamic Terrorism") applied by the West to Islam, thus became a self–fulfilling prophecy among such marginal groups. It is important to note here that "Muslim" and "Islam" are not labels. Islam signifies a state of affairs, a complete submission to God's will as contained in the Koran. The Koran condemns all forms of terrorism and war directed against civilians and non–aggressors.

The Koran is explicit on the freedom of conscience:

> *"There is no compulsion in religion. Truth is clear from falsehood (Koran 2:256)*

> *"You are in no way a tyrant or forcer over them; but warn by the Koran him who fears my threat (Koran 50:45)."*

History gives a lie to the "fairy tale" that Islam spread by the sword:

• Muslims ruled over Spain for 736 years. If the Muslims had used any force during those 736 years to convert the Christians to Islam there wouldn't have been a single Christian left to kick out the Muslims after 736 years of rule.

• Over 150 million Muslims live in Indonesia, yet no Muslim army ever invaded any of its over 2000 islands. Similar is the case with Malaysia, and the east coast of Africa. Odd instances of "Muslims" not guided by the Koran, forcing people to accept their "Islam" may be found. Similar cases can be found in Christianity or with any other religions group.

"Charlemagne's conversion of the saxons to Christianity was not by preaching." (THOMAS CARLYLE, ON HEROES AND HERO WORSHIP, 1918: 80)

Theory and action need to be separated for the purpose of pure research. Islam should be judged based on its "system doctrine" found only in the Koran and not "Muslim" action. Bad "Muslims" don't condemn Islam, just like bad Christians don't condemn Christianity. Hitler was a self proclaimed Christian. Do his acts condemn Christianity?

"My feelings as a Christian points me to my Lord and Savior as a fighter. It points me to the man who once in loneliness, surrounded by a few followers, recognized these Jews for what they were and summoned men to fight against them and who, God's truth! was greatest not as a sufferer but as a fighter. In boundless love as a Christian and as a man I read through the passage which tells us how the Lord at last rose in His might and seized the scourge to drive out of the Temple the brood of vipers and adders. How terrific was His fight for the world against the Jewish poison. To–day, after two thousand years, with deepest emotion I recognize more profoundly than ever before the fact that it was for this that He had to shed His blood upon the Cross. As a Christian I have no duty to allow myself to be cheated, but I have the duty to be a fighter for truth and justice… And if there is anything which could demonstrate that we are acting rightly it is the distress that daily grows. For as a Christian I have also a duty to my own people.–Adolf Hitler, in a speech on 12 April 1922 (Norman H. Baynes, ed. The Speeches of Adolf Hitler, April 1922–August 1939, Vol. 1 of 2, pp. 19–20, Oxford University Press, 1942)

History is clear:

"History makes it clear however that the legend of fanatical Muslims sweeping through the world and forcing Islam at the

*point of the sword upon conquered races is one of the most fantasti-
cally absurd myths that historians ever repeated." (DE LACY O`
LEARY, ISLAM AT THE CROSS ROADS, LONDON 1923)*

*"The greatest success of Muhammad's life was effected by sheer
moral force without the stroke of a sword." (EDWARD GIBBON,
HISTORY OF THE SARACEAN EMPIRE, LONDON 1817)*

iii) Peace and Islam

The word Islam comes from the Arabic root word *salaam*, which means
peace. The universal greeting of Muslims is *"As Salaam o Aleykum"*. It
means: "peace be with you." The Koran, the only book of authority on
Islam encourages peace making among humankind.

The idea of a "United Nations" working for world peace is actually bor-
rowed from the Koran:

> *"There is no good in much of their secret conferences except, him
> who enjoins alms giving and kindness and **peace making** among
> mankind. Whoever does that seeking the good pleasure of God?
> God will bestow on him (her) a vast reward (Koran 4:114)."*

Islam gives a worldview of a close relationship between all men &
women based on a common essence of creation (Koran 4:1)and only one
creator God.

> *"O Humankind! We have created you males and females, and
> have divided you into nations and tribes so that you may recog-
> nize each other. The best among you in the sight of God is the one
> most careful [of the truth] (Koran 49:13)."*

Source:

Asadi, Muhammed. *The Truth About Jihad* (http:// members.aol.com
/silence004/jihad.htm).

3

The Koran and Women

*"O Humankind! We have created you **male and female** and have divided you into nations and tribes that you recognize each other. The best of you in the sight of God is the one most socially aware (**taqwa** in Arabic) Koran 49:13*

The Liberated Woman:

We see some common characteristics in modern urban culture concerning what is required of men and women: Open chest shirts for the female, a necktie for the male. Belly exposed shirts for the female, tucked–in shirts for the male. Men's dress patronizes opaque clothing where as feminine clothes are transparent. Modern society labels a man as improperly dressed when not in full suit but women are celebrated if they keep their legs uncovered, even on a cold winter night.

The society that condemns the exhibition of male physical curves and labels them as "perversion" provides artificial aides to under developed areas of the female. Everyone has heard the term, "unwed mother" but you hardly ever hear about the "unwed father" The fashion world usually controlled by males, aims to create instability in the female mind. She is taught that "wearing the least" is something that builds "status" and taking it all off is "liberation".

She is taught to hate her own body. The form of her eyelashes and brows, the style of her walking and speech, the color of her lips, nails and cheek are all given an artificial look. She also hates the natural trend of her hair (Omer 1989). In such a society, hair fashion designers, cosmetic manufacturers, and plastic surgeons make big money. Where men balance themselves on a three–inch base heel of the shoes, the woman is expected to balance herself on a half a centimeter heel, creating a medical abnormality. Males make big money, displaying female nakedness through their "respectable" trades like cabarets, strip bars, fashion shows, and especially commercial advertising (Do I want the Mustang or the sexy blonde in the advertisement?), nude paintings magazines and internet web pages.

Modern western culture does not only show the above but it also shows alarming statistics of single parents, children with no fathers, broken families, sex crimes, divorce, suicide and drug use among teens, asylums for unclaimed children, homes for unwanted parents, clinics for delinquent youth and neurotic adults. Recent estimates suggest that up to 80% of US society displays some form or the other of psychological symptoms, and that up to 22% have psychological problems serious enough to interfere with their day to day living, which are diagnosable (Chicago Tribune 12/1999).

Data in the United States also shows that 25 to 35 percent of girls are sexually abused, usually by men well known to them (Kilbourne 1999:253). A high percentage of women so assaulted suffer from Post Traumatic Stress Disorder (the same disorder that a large number of Vietnam veterans suffer from) that leads to addiction and substance abuse and eventually to poverty and homelessness.

In such societies "liberation" of women has been reduced to a slogan to sell products. Such sellers of "liberation", mostly men, offer women "liberation" via smoking, alcohol, food and their natural longing for stable relationships (which have dwindled in such a society). This commercial "liberation" comes at a great cost to women and serves to isolate them through addiction. As addicts make great consumers, the sellers of such "liberation" want to keep it that way (Kilbourne 1999).

When such sellers of "liberation" are faced with true demands for gender equality, like the ERA (Equal Rights Amendment in the United States), they reject them outright and a government funded and controlled by them makes it fail (ERA failed to pass in 1982). Such powers that be in these societies, not only attack any true efforts towards liberation of women in their own society (as they are commercially disadvantageous to them), but also attack all other ideas presented as truly liberating to women, by other societies (to which they export their commercial culture) by labeling them, "harsh, barbaric, and primitive". They do this through their control of the media, and the support of groups that deliberately project what they want to present as "evidence". The media, if not owned by them, directly depends on them, through their advertising dollars, for its very survival (Kilbourne 1999).

This paper is an attempt to rewrite the history of women's rights and to clarify the position of a book, the Koran on a subject, which has been deliberately distorted and misrepresented through the ages.

WOMEN IN WESTERN RELIGION:

Christianity, the major religion that shaped western thought, presents women as subordinate to men. Men according to the Bible are the owners of women, just like an animal is owned. Exodus 20:17 which states the famous tenth commandment, lumps a wife together with his servants, animals and house. A man could sell his daughter as a slave (Exodus 21:7–11) or give her in marriage to whomsoever he chose.

This subordination of women to men in the Bible, which shaped western thought on the issue, is made clear in Leviticus 12:1–8: After the birth of a male child, a woman is ritually impure for seven days, however after the birth of a female child, she is ritually impure for fourteen according to this law of the Bible.

1 Corinthians 14:34–35 of the New Testament of the Bible states:

"As in all Churches of the saints, the woman should be subordinate as even the Law says…for it is shameful for a woman to speak in church."

1 Timothy 2:11 states:

"Let a woman learn in silence with all submissiveness. I permit no woman to teach or have authority over men. She is to keep silent, for Adam was formed first then Eve, and Adam was not deceived but the woman was deceived and became a transgressor."

1 Corinthians 11:6 says:

"For if a woman will not veil herself then she should cut off her hair, but if it is disgraceful for a woman to be shorn or shaven, let her wear a veil…for man was not created from woman but woman from man. Neither was man created for woman but woman for man."

Jesus' track record, based on the New Testament, isn't much better in his treatment of women, even his own mother. According to the Gospel of John, he is openly rude to his mother. Having become famous among the people, according to John or whoever wrote the Gospel of John, he addresses his mother in this rude manner:

"Woman! What have I to do with you. My time is not yet (John 2:8)."

Imagine, if you're a woman and your son or your daughter said, "Woman! What have I to do with you", how you would feel? Considering a mother's sacrifice and discomfort in bearing and delivering a child, such behavior is unacceptable. Hardly an exemplary character that Christian evangelists depict the "Prince of peace" had. The Koran states:

"Be grateful to God AND the wombs that bore you."(Koran 4:1)

Your mother bore you in discomfort over discomfort…"(Koran 31:14)

The Koran disputes with the idea that the gospels are a genuine account of the words of Jesus, as do the scholars of the Jesus Seminar, based on modern findings. Contrary to what the Gospels present Jesus as saying to his mother, the Koran quotes him as saying:

> *"And God has made me kind and dutiful towards my mother and not arrogant or overbearing (Koran 19:32)."*

Helen Ellerbe, in her book, *The Dark Side of Christian History* (1995) elaborates on the Church's (both Catholic and Protestant) treatment of women:

> *The second century St. Clement of Alexandria wrote: "Every woman should be filled with shame by the thought that she is a woman." The Church father Tertullian explained why women deserve their status as despised and inferior human beings:*
>
> > *You are the devil's gateway: you are the unsealer of the tree: you are the first deserter of the divine law…You destroyed so easily God's image, man. On account of your desert–that is, death–even the Son of God had to die [Joan Smith, Misogynies: Reflections on Myths and Malice (N.Y Fawcett Columbine, 1989:66)].*
>
> *Others expressed the view more bluntly. The sixth century Christian philosopher, Boethius, wrote in The Consolation of Philosophy, "Woman is a temple built upon a sewer." Bishops in the sixth century council of Macon voted as to whether women had souls. In the tenth century, Odo of Cluny declared, " To embrace a woman is to embrace a sack of manure…"The thir-teenth century St. Thomas Aquinas suggested that God had made a mistake in creating woman: "Nothing deficient [or defective] should have been produced in the first establishment of things; so women ought not to have been produced then." And Lutherans at Wittenberg debated whether women were really human beings at all. Orthodox Christians held women responsible for all sin. As the [Roman Catholic] Bible Apocrypha states, "Of woman came the beginning of sin/ And thanks to her we all must die*

(Ecclesiasticus 25:13–26)."...As 1 Corinthians 7:1 states, "It is a good thing for man to have nothing to do with a woman."

The 1500s marked the beginning of "witchcraft persecutions." By the 1700s over 100,000 people, 80–90 percent of them women, had been put to death in Europe, usually by burning at the stake (Chicago Tribune Dec 29, 1999–A profile of women's history). This amounted to be a self–fulfilling prophecy, as the religious King James I estimated that the ratio of women to men who "succumbed" to witchcraft was twenty to one (Ellerby 1995:116).

Keeping a woman silent according to what St. Paul had said was widely practiced in Europe and the Christian world. In 1833 when the first coeducational college in The U.S, Oberlin College was established, women were not allowed to speak in many classes. In 1623 in England, a woman sentenced by a court to be "too frank" was publicly displayed in a "scold bridle", i.e. a metal cage around her head with a spiked plate which cut her tongue if she dared speak.

Contrary to this God, in the Koran, not only encourages women to speak, but says that they are listened to and admonishes men to be fair and just with them. Consider this statement in the Koran :

> *"God hears the saying of her who argues with you concerning her husband, and complains to God. God hears your mutual complaints...(Koran 57:1)"*

HINDUISM AND WOMEN:

In Hindu religious literature by far, the most effective weapon used by the gods to corrupt virtuous mortals is a woman. Usually a seductive celestial nymph but sometimes, just woman, the root of all evil in the ascetic oriented view of the orthodox Hindu (Baldick, Radice, Jones 1975:36).

The Mahabharata states, " *I will tell you my son, how Brahma created wanton women and for what purpose, for there is nothing more evil than women... The Lord Grandfather, learning what was in the hearts of the Gods,*

created wanton women by a magic ritual in order to delude mankind."
(13.40.3–10)

The complete subservience of wives to their husbands in Hindu custom shows up in the practice of Sati, where the wife burns herself alive on her dead husbands pyre. In 1780, when the Raja of Marwar died in India, his 64 wives burned themselves alive on his funeral pyre. Even though the secular government of India made this practice illegal, it still continues to be practiced because of religion.

CHINESE RELIGIOUS CONCEPTS AND WOMEN:

The Yin and the Yang is a concept quite familiar even in the west especially in merchandise. In their mythical theory of how the universe operates, Chinese philosophers invented the concept of the Yin and Yang. The universe they concluded is understood to be a balance of the Yin (evil or negative) and the Yang (good or positive).

When asked to further describe Yin (evil), the explanation comes:

> *"The Yin is the negative force in nature. It is seen in darkness, coolness, **femaleness** dampness, the earth, moon and the shadows. The Yang (good) is the positive force in nature. It is seen in lightness, warmness, **maleness**, dryness and the sun (Hopfe 1991:207)."*

Max Weber, the German sociologist, recognized and known for his work on the Sociology of Religion, writes in his work on Confusianism and Taoism:

> *The doctrine held in common by ALL schools of philosophy [in Chinese Religion] summarised the "good" spirits as the [heavenly and masculine] Yang principle, the "evil" ones as the [earthly and feminine] Yin principle, explaining the origin of the world from their fusion (Ed. Gerth 1951:29)*

Until 1901, the Chinese practiced "foot binding" for girls, which deformed the girl's feet. It had been practiced for around a thousand years, based on tradition, till it was banned in 1901. Even after being banned, it was widely practiced until 1949. Marie Vento (1998), in her paper, *One Thousand Years of Chinese Footbinding: Its Origins, Popularity and Demise* (retrieved from the Internet 01/15/'00), writes:

> *In its most extreme form, footbinding was the act of wrapping a three–to five–year old girl's feet with binding so as to bend the toes under, break the bones and force the back of the foot together. Its purpose was to produce a tiny foot, the "golden lotus", which was three inches long and thought to be both lovely and alluring...*

> *One notable personality who aided in the spread of footbinding was the famed writer and scholar Zhu Xi (1130–1200 A.D), whose commentaries on the Confucian classics would form the canon of Neo–Confucianism that would dominate Chinese intellectual and philosophical life for six subsequent centuries. An ardent advocate of footbinding, he introduced the practice into southern Fuijan in order to spread Chinese culture and teach proper relations between men and women, greatly influencing other writers who mention the practice as if it were normal...For men footbinding is troubling because it suggests not only that men are capable of perceiving a gruesomely crippled foot as an object of seductive pleasure, but that they are further capable of using their superior social position to coerce women to conform to a standard of beauty that is both deformed and grotesque. For women, foot-binding is unsettling because it reveals a willingness to cripple their own daughters to meet an aesthetic and criterion of social behavior defined by men."*

FEMALE INFANTICIDE AND
HINDU AND CHINESE TRADITION:

Not only did the Koran outlaw female infanticide, which was widely practiced in Arabia at the time of the prophet Muhammed, it made it an issue to be especially addressed on Judgment Day:

"And when the girl–child buried alive is asked for what sin she was killed..."

(Koran 81:8–9)

The Koran places extreme importance on every single human life, be it male or female, of whatever color or nationality. The statement of the Koran reproduced below on the dignity of every single life is unsurpassed in world literature. The Koran states, without differentiating between male, female, race, religion or nationality:

"...Whosoever kills even one human being, other than man slaughter or tyranny on earth, it would be as if he had killed all of humanity. And whosoever saves even one human life, it will be as if they have saved all of humankind (Koran 5:32)"

Not only is female infanticide widely practiced in India based on the traditional Hindu preference for male children compared to females (resulting in over 10,000 confirmed cases every year–non reported cases are many more), modern technology is being used to abort female fetuses (Naft & Levine 1997:304–307).

Naft and Levine (1997) write in their International Report on the Status of Women:

"...Yet since the mid 1970s, when parents found that modern medical techniques could determine the sex of a fetus and enable them to identify and abort female fetuses, the practice has become commonplace...Government officials even suspect that the disproportionate abortion of female fetuses may be a major underlying

cause of the recent decline in the nation's sex ratio." (Naft &
Levine 1997:304–305)

There is a strong preference among traditional Chinese for boys instead of girls. Until 1992 there was no law in China that outlawed female infanticide. Give the "one child law" and the traditional preference for male children, female infanticide was commonly practiced and resulted in the famous "missing girl" problem in China (Naft & Levine 1997).

THE KORAN AND WOMEN:

> *"And among God's signs is this: He created for you mates from amongst yourselves (males as mates for females and vice versa) that you might find tranquillity and peace in them. And he has put love and kindness among you. Herein surely are signs for those who reflect (Koran 30:21)."*

Surprisingly egalitarian in its approach, given its time of origin, the Koran doesn't agree with the Biblical idea of men being the owners of women, neither does it agree with women being created for or from men like the Bible nor does it say that women cannot teach or have authority over men. The Koran also dispels the common myth among other religions in general that a woman is evil by nature and has been created to deceive mankind. The purpose, says the Koran, of mates is that tranquillity and peace emerges through the natural instinct of love and kindness among mates.

People who analyze the Koran however sometimes feel differently about many of its verses, which to them suggest that the Koran is in some way putting down women. These verses are a handful and given the nature of this chapter, we can go in detail with them.

The verse in the Koran that causes trouble to most liberals and is misused by evangelical Christians is:

> *"Men are the protectors (Qawamoon) of women, because God has given preference to some over others. And because men spend*

of their property on women. So good women are obedient, guard-
ing even unnoticed that what Allah (God) has asked them to
guard. As for those from whom you fear rebellion in this (i.e.
guarding their chastity in your absence), i) talk to them, ii) leave
them alone in their beds, iii) strike them. If they then obey you,
look not for any way against them... (Koran 4:34)."

The verse in question is quite clear if we don't jump to hasty conclusions. Men have been given the duty to protect and support women. God
has given preference to one gender over another in certain duties. Men
have been given preference in being the providers of women and women
are given preference in caring for a child. Even if divorce separates a man
from his wife, he has to seek her help in caring for the child or another
female if the mother agrees (Koran 2:233). Men are told to spend of their
property on women and not ask the woman for anything, even if she happens to be rich.

Now to the controversial part: The verse asks women to guard even when
unnoticed, that which God has asked them to guard. If we have read the
Koran carefully, we won't have trouble in determining that God specifically
asks women and men to "guard" their chastity (Koran 24:30–31). To the
women who cheat on their husbands, the Koran gives a three step, braking
mechanism to hasty divorce or worse still capital punishment for adultery.

Step one, the husband should talk to the wife and try to resolve it.
Usually, given men's image in popular culture, step one would be shouting
and cursing and maybe even hitting. Around four million women in the
US are severally battered each year. Two to four thousand of them die,
according to conservative estimates. Rather unfortunate and avoidable if a
braking mechanism exists for people exercising their emotions. Contrary
to this, the Koran suggests that talk be the first option.

Step two, the Koran recommends that marital relations be temporarily
stopped between the couple, if cheating persists even after a talk. This
would give the woman further opportunity to consider if she wants to separate from the man and provide for herself after divorce or if she'd rather

stay in the current marriage. If however the couple want to separate, which most people would if there was cheating going on, the Koran states in the next verse:

> *"And if you fear a breach between the two (husband and wife),*
> *appoint an arbiter from his family and an arbiter from her family.*
> *If they (husband and wife) desire amendment, God will make them*
> *of one mind. For God is knowing and is aware (Koran4: 35)."*

If however the woman wants to stay with the man but doesn't quit cheating, i.e. break up the extra marital relationship, then the Koran says resort to Step three, which is implicitly for the woman's own benefit especially in an economically harsh environment. Step three, the Koran says strike them. The word used signifies a single symbolic hit. The word hit in the verse does not represent "beating up" in any way. It is not supposed to injure the woman but is meant to be symbolic. Thus the same word **Darab,** is used in the Koran to "strike or hit" someone with an example, **Darab al masl.** If it injures the woman, than the woman according to Islamic law can have the authorities retaliate against the man, as he would have broken the law, as for injury there is equal retaliation according to the Koran (5:45).

Here is the situation that warrants step three: the woman doesn't want to end the current marriage and also doesn't want to put an end to her cheating episodes, the Koran suggests that the husband strike her, for her own benefit. This is very liberal. The woman on her own would be under financial hardship and so she wants to use the current marital relationship. However she also doesn't want to quit cheating on her husband. People, men or women, normally aren't so forgiving so as to keep the marriage and accept that the other party remains cheating. Something has to be done to make the relationship compatible, *after* both talking and temporarily halting marital relationship hasn't worked. However, in all sincerity, I can state confidently that step 3 will never arrive since both the man and the woman are free to end the relationship during the course of step 1 and step 2.

The Koran by making the symbolic hit step 3 is actually controlling human emotions of anger, which frequently comes before talking and reasoning given popular culture. It makes it virtually impossible that a man going through 1 and 2 will resort to 3 also and not break the marriage before. Where there are difficulties that need to be settled, the Koran provides a very modern and just arbitration system (see Koran 4:35 above). The Koran is concerned to the utmost about women's rights. Human society has usually not given equal opportunity to women, even today in the West. The Koran wants to protect women in a harsh society and at the same time change men's "control–oriented" minds to one that are more reasonable. The method the Koran uses is more result oriented than dogmatic, where both parties are dealt with equitably and with justice.

By making hitting step 3 the Koran effectively controls the anger emotion that is often spontaneous in such situations. Good reasoning and communication, arbitration to settle differences and short suspension of marital relations should effectively do away with any tendency to hit. The Koran is thus not just putting a count of ten between a man and his anger, but days and weeks. It thus gives anger and mistrust a long time and a systematic procedure to get resolved.

Compare the Koran's breaking mechanism for controlling anger to the fact that wife beating was not outlawed in the United States until 1871 (over 13 centuries after the Koran). Even after being outlawed, in the absence of such procedures contained in the Koran, domestic violence affects at least a third of all women in the United States, over four million annually [this figure is over 80% under represented as most cases go unreported] (Newman 1998). According to the FBI Uniform Crime Report of 1991, it is the leading cause of injury to women 15 to 44. Over a third of women who die in the United States die at the hands of husbands or boyfriends (Kilbourne 1999). I can confidently state that if such a procedure as the Koran presented was internalized, not only would women not get injured, there would be more talking and communication and little or no violence at home. The system of the Koran works where just saying, "Don't do it" would not and has not.

This attitude of the Koran to protect women in an economically harsh environment is seen in many places throughout the book. For example, men married to women who then become guilty of lesbianism or bisexuality are told not to throw the women out of their homes but to keep them there till some way is found (Koran 24:3).

The Koran has given some duty preference to men over women and some to women over men. This was mentioned briefly before. However, this doesn't mean that the Koran forbids women from earning their livelihood, if they want to. Koran 4:22 for example states that for men is what they earn and for women what they earn and that both men and women should seek God's bounty collectively.

PROPERTY LAWS:

Around two hundred years back, women had no property rights in Europe. Islam has given them such since the start. Before the 1840s women had no property rights in America. Property rights in Islam, given the nature of the various relationships that man and women fit under, are surprisingly egalitarian. When a man marries a woman, he has to give a substantial part of his property (according to his means) to the woman as a "marriage gift (*Mahar*)," stated as a man's duty unto God (Koran 4:24).

A woman doesn't have to give anything to a man even if she is rich. It is for this reason primarily that the Koran asks that out of a parents property the son get twice that of the daughter (Koran 4:11). It is expected that the daughter would marry and get a man's property as marriage gift and not have to worry about providing for herself, as it's the man's duty to provide for her. The son on the other hand would Islamically be expected not only to provide for his potential wife but also give a major part of his property to her as marriage gift.

This however, is not discrimination among the genders. There are specific reasons why the son gets twice that of the daughter. When the conditions are different, the Koran suggests that both male and female get the same amount. For example out of a son's wealth both the father (male) and the mother (female) get equal shares if the deceased had a son.

LEGAL BATTLES:

"O believers. When you contract a debt for a given fixed term, record it in writing…and call to witnesses from among your men, two witnesses. And if two men be not present then one man and two women of such as you approve as witnesses, so that if one of them errs, the other admonishes her (Koran 2:82)."

Both faithful believers and attackers from all camps have abused this particular statement in the Koran. It is presented by them in a generalized form with a concluding statement that Islam considers women's testimony to be half that of men.

The above verse does not talk about testimony in general but only presents one case basically involving financial transactions. It doesn't state any generalization of women's testimony being half that of men, or that two women will equal one man. If interpretation is sought, then a positive one would be that the Koran wants to protect women from being unfairly influenced or pressurized by men. As support for the woman, another woman is supplemented, so that if one errs the other reminds her.

The Koran recognizes this difference in men and women, be it social or biological and corrects for it to support the woman from being manipulated by men. The end purpose is justice, which shouldn't offend any reasonable person. In different circumstances however, one woman's testimony is given more weight, where it concerns herself, than one man's testimony in the Koran, as it can override it. This case would be when a man (husband) accuses a woman (his wife) of cheating in a relationship but has no witness except his own testimony, which is against her testimony (Koran 24:6–9). The Koran gives women's testimony more weight than a man's!

DRESS:

We read above that the Bible recommends that women veil themselves or shave off their hair. Contrary to what Muslim practice has been for many centuries, the Koran does not ask women to cover themselves from head to toe. Contrary to that, it states:

> "Tell the believing men to lower their gaze and guard their chastity; that is purer for them. And tell the believing women to lower their gaze and guard their chastity, and not to make a display of their beauty except what is apparent, and let them cast a cover over their bosoms.... And turn to Allah (God) altogether, O believers, in order that you might succeed (Koran 24: 30–31)."

The Koran suggests that *both men and women* dress modestly and guard their chastity. Other than that, the Koran suggests that women put a covering on their chest (bosom) over the regular clothing they wear and not make a wanton display of their beauty (Koran 24:30–31). This does not fit in any way the picture of a woman wearing a *chador* or *burka* (veil) covered from head to toe. It would more closely resemble a picture of a woman wearing a shirt and pants, which do not deliberately reveal her body, with a extra cover over her chest (bosom) only.

Tradition and not the Koran made "tradition based" Muslims bring the veil into Islam from Christian custom (see Paul's saying on the veil). The Koran did not sanction it. The statement in the Koran that talks about dress, talks about both men and women dressing modestly, guarding their chastity and lowering their gaze. It does not discriminate between the sexes except in the case of women it asks them to take a extra covering over their bosoms (chest) only.

POLYGAMY AND THE KORAN:

Two things that come to mind whenever Islam or the Koran is mentioned in the West (in relation to women) are Islamic polygamy and the restrictive Islamic dress for women (the infamous veil). A third thing also commonly crops up when talking about Islam in general and that is terrorism (Jihad or so–called holy war). These three effectively describe the stereotype of Islam held by the West. Like most stereotypes they are based either on ignorance or describe the practice of those that base their actions on tradition other than the Koran. Instead of attacking tradition, those with vested interests attack Islam and the Koran.

There is nothing in Christianity or Judaism against polygamy (polygyny–one man taking more than one wife). Indeed the Old Testament assumes that marriages will be polygamous and laws are constructed based on that assumption. For example, Exodus 21:10 in the Bible states:

> "If he take to him another wife, her food, her raiment, and her duty of marriage shall he not diminish." (The Bible, Exodus 21:10)

There is not a word attributed to Jesus in the New Testament which disallows polygamy. Paul forbade bishops and deacons from marrying more than one wife (1 Timothy 3:2), this implicitly suggests that other were allowed polygamy (polygyny). The insistence on monogamy was an invention introduced by the Roman Catholic Church as late as AD 600 just as the invention of the celibacy of the clergy, the Church being against marriage in general and not only polygamy (Cairncross 1974:70). The early Lutheran Church in Munster, Germany proclaimed polygamy (polygyny) the "ideal form of marriage" (Cairncross 1974:1)

Any mention of polygamy in the West today, among feminists and non–feminists alike evokes feeling of hate. This hate is rooted in Western culture and not religion as we have seen above. The culture that hates polygamy however allows all sexual intercourse between a man and a woman in plurality (as long as it is pre or non–marital).

However the same intercourse made "responsible" by marriage in the plural is outlawed and hated.

The Koran severely restricted the open practice of polygamy. The statement in the Koran that deals with polygamy is just one yet it is misused and abused by both Muslims and Non–Muslims. It states:

> *"And if you fear that you will not be able to deal justly with the oppressed women [Yatama–literally, the Orphans among women], then marry from among them two or three or four, but if you fear you wont be just [even then], then marry only one (Koran 4:3)."*

The Koran states explicitly above that polygyny is allowed *only* if the women you marry:

1. Belong among oppressed (orphan) women. Men *cannot* pick and choose from "any" women who they want as a second wife.

2. Polygamy is to practiced only if marriage would bring social justice to such women (*"if you fear that you will not be able to deal justly,"* says the Koran), justice that they are otherwise denied.

3. If marrying more than one cannot bring such justice then polygamy is not allowed. Thus the Koran severely restricts and restricted in Arabia, the open practice of polygamy in society.

The Koran does not, like the early Lutheran Church, term polygamy the "ideal" form. According to the Koran, polygamy is a good option only when it brings social justice to the oppressed classes of women.

According to poverty expert William Julius Wilson (1996), 31% of the continually poor in America comprise of "non–elderly" African American women. Now these are among the oppressed classes of women. If polygamy by well established men could bring social justice to them by removing their children and hence future generations from this "cycle of poverty," it is good. It is also recognized by many sociologists and by Dr. Wilson himself that "non–marriage" and the "lack of marriage" is a viable reason in their poverty and status. "Lack or marriage" or a "broken house-hold" is recognized universally by sociologists as contributing to such poverty. It is recognized that divorce and out of wedlock childbearing has resulted in the "feminization of poverty (Schaefer 2000)." In Iraq after the Gulf War, when thousands of women became widows, restricted polygamy by just individuals would similarly have been very functional.

A country like the United States where the population of women is a few million more than the population of men, especially at older ages, some women can statistically never find husbands if everyone practiced monogamy. Such oppressed women, facing a double jeopardy of sexism and ageism, could be given family life and hence social and economic justice by "restricted" Koranic polygamy, in a male–dominated society.

The Koran is well aware that men misuse polygamy as they are "swayed by the greed of their hearts" (Koran 4:128), and thus puts severe restrictions on the practice of polygamy to protect the rights of women and wives. As a result the oldest monotheistic "religious" book that states explicitly, *"…then marry only one* (Koran 4:3)" is the Koran. Monogamy is prescribed for society in general with "restricted" polygamy being allowed when special circumstances warrant it.

DIVORCE:

The Koran by giving women a right to initiate divorce is truly revolutionary. The New Testament, in the supposed words of Jesus, makes divorce an offense similar to adultery, permissible only when the woman has cheated on the husband (Matthew 5:32). The Old Testament states that only a man can initiate divorce (Deuteronomy 24:1).

The Koran, contrary to that states:

> *"…If you both fear that you wont be able to keep within the boundaries of God in marriage, there is no harm if SHE ransom herself…" (Koran 2:229)*

The ransom would of course be the return of the initial property that the man gave her when she got married to him (*the Mahar*).

It is a common misconception that Islam offers a quick divorce. If the man says, "I divorce you," three times to the woman, the marriage is nullified, according to popular rumor. This is not true. The Koran offers an elaborate braking system for divorce. A system which is so advanced for its time that it is now being suggested in England to stop careless "quick" divorce, which creates a burden on both the adults and children in question.

The Koran's method of divorce is simple yet very functional. If mind is set on divorce, a divorce statement is written and pronounced in the presence of witnesses (Koran 65:2). Then there is a three month break in which both parties stay together as husband and wife, so that time be given to reconsider (Koran 2:228). After the three–month period, if the man initiated the divorce, he can either take the wife back, if she wants to remain in the marriage, or part. If he takes her back he can initiate divorce only once more in his life with the same woman. If he takes her back the second time, then he has lost his rights to initiate divorce in the same relationship ever again (Koran 2:229). A woman can buyout her divorce by surrendering the property that was given her by the husband, whenever she thinks the marriage wont work out. All through this process, the Koran suggest that help be sought by arbitration (Koran 4:35), one person from the man's side and one from the woman's. Very modern concepts given the history of the Koran.

Yet, the same culture that points fingers at Islam for its "quick" divorce has a divorce rate of over 50 percent. Out of every hundred new marriages in the United States over fifty (old or new) will end in divorce.

Regarding divorce, since the man has been providing for the woman, regardless of who initiated the *divorce* proceedings, the Koran states:

> "*...And for women are rights equal to the rights against them, in what is just. However men have a degree over them (in the context of divorce only–read the context) (2:228).*"

It is very clear that this verse is stating that there can be *no absolute equal laws* when conditions on both sides differ. *Giving equal laws under unequal circumstances would be injustice.* The Koran wants equality with justice. Thus women are allowed to divorce a man once (by surrendering the property the man gave her) and the husband can initiate the divorce twice.

Not only is the Koran the only "religious" book that explicitly states, *"and for women are rights equal to the rights against them in justice (2:228)"*, it is more egalitarian than modern laws.

As late as 1982 in the United States for example, the Equal Rights Amendment that called for equal rights for men and women in the law, failed. The Koran truly liberated women over fourteen hundred years back declaring that for women will be rights equal to those against them in justice! *Koran: A Defender of Women's Rights:*

> *"And when you men have divorced women, …then either retain them in kindness if you reconcile, or part with them in kindness. Do not retain them to harm them so that you transgress limits. He who does this has wronged himself (Koran 2:231)."*

> *"O believers! It is not lawful for you to inherit women against their will, nor that you should put restrictions on them, that you might take what you had given them…Consort with them in kindness, for if you hate them, it might happen that you hate something in which God has put much good (Koran 4:19)."*

Men and Women Together:

> *"Women impure for men impure. And men impure for women impure. Women of purity for men of purity, and men of purity for women of purity. These are not affected by what people say. For them is forgiveness and an honorable provision (Koran 24:26)."*

"And their Lord has heard them and says: 'I don't let the work of any worker be lost be they male or female. You both proceed one from the other..(Koran 3:195)."

"Indeed, men who submit and women who submit, believing men and believing women, and men who obey and women who obey, and truthful men and truthful women, and men who persevere and women who persevere, and men who are humble and women who are humble, and men who give alms and women who give alms, and men who fast and women who fast, and men who guard their chastity and women who guard their chastity, and men who remember God much and women who remember God much. God has prepared for them forgiveness and a great reward (Koran 33:35)."

"And the believers men and women are friends one of the other, they enjoin what is right and forbid what is wrong, and they establish worship and pay the poor due, and they obey God and his messenger. As for these, God will have mercy on them…(Koran 9:71)."

Women as Examples for Men and Women:

*"God cites an **example** for those who believe: the wife of Pharaoh when she said: My Lord! Build for me a home with you in the Garden, and deliver me from Pharaoh and his work and save me from a tyrannous people. And Mary the daughter of Emran, who guarded her chastity, and we inspired in her of our spirit. She confirmed the words of her God and his books and was of the steadfast (Koran 66: 11–12)."*

While reading the above statements in the Koran take note of the fact that men and women are mentioned together as "equals" in status. This concept is repeated time and again in the Koran based on the common origin of humankind (Koran 4:1). Unlike the Bible, the Koran does not accept the idea that woman are created from or for man. As a result, a common notion that is repeated in the Koran is, *"…You (men and women) proceed one from the other (3:195 etc)."*

Summary:

Most people may not have any idea on what Islam is or what it stands for but they are all "experts" on the oppressed woman in Islam. After reading the contents of this paper, it should be evident that:

1. Islam is the only religion that gives equal rights to everyone regardless of race or sex. There is no religious book, not even the constitution of the US, which states explicitly like the Koran, *"And for women are rights equal to the rights against them in justice."*

2. The Koran does not ask women to veil themselves completely from head to toe. Such may be Muslim practice in many parts of the world, but it is not sanctioned by the Koran. The Koran merely asks both men and women to dress modestly and not to flout their nakedness. On the other hand, the Bible which many claim Western civilization was based on, demands that women wear the veil (1 Corinthians11: 6) or risk having their head shaven.

3. Men and women are of equal human status in the Koran (Koran 3:195), however Christian doctrine on which the early American societies were based, had Biblical norms which hold that a woman is subordinate to a man (1 Corinthians 14:34) and are created for man (1 Timothy 2:11)

4. Islam based on the Koran which is very different to the Islam that Muslim masses believe in, gave women the right to property ownership and a voice in legal testimony centuries before such "revolutionary" ideas were even dreamed of by Europeans and their US counterparts.

5. The Koran prescribes polygamy only among the oppressed classes of women, if marriage can better their status in society and is just and equitable. If marriage cannot provide justice to the woman, then the Koran

prescribes monogamy as the only option. The only "religious" book that explicitly states, *"then marry only one (Koran 4:3)"*, is the Koran.

6. Within the text of the Koran the ignorant practice of female circumcision, which many people believe is the norm in Islam, is not even mentioned. It is an innovation in Islam, not something that the Koran suggested or prescribed. It is not a part of Islam or the Koran.

7. Islam has never had a problem with women in authority. Even today, Muslim lands have female heads of states. We have yet to see a woman president in the US.

The cure for Sexism and Racism:

> *"O Humankind! We have created you male and female and have divided you into nations and tribes that you recognize each other. The best of you in the sight of God is the one most socially aware (**taqwa**–literally it means "extremely careful")." Koran 49:13*

Division into sexes and nations is merely for the purpose of recognition and has nothing to do with status or one being better than the other, according to the Koran.

> *"And of God's signs is the creation of the heavens and the earth, and the difference in your **colors and languages**. Indeed in this are signs for those who have knowledge." Koran 30:22*

Just like the different languages in the world, the different colors of humankind are a sign of God. They have nothing to do with status of one or the other being better based on language or color.

This chapter does not at all try to defend *Sunni* or *Shia* Islam. The "Islam" believed in by the masses of Muslims (which I refer to as "tradition based" Islam), includes with the Koran other authorities in their "religion". These authorities are *Hadith* [sayings attributed to the prophet] and *fiqh* [so called Islamic jurisprudence]. These sources are not warranted by the Koran and entered Islam centuries after the death of the prophet, in the form that we have today (for details see http://www.rationalreality.com).

They were based on oral traditions unlike the Koran, which was written down from day one. In these "extra–Koranic" sources we find many statements that are derogatory of women and giving them a lower status compared to men. Some statements in the *hadith* for example compare women to monkeys and dogs and call them bad luck. They even suggest that the woman serve her husband like a "lesser–god". Not only is this outrageous, it goes against the strict monotheism of the Koran. The Koran is the only book of authority in Islam.

Bibliography:

1.   *The Koran*: translated from the Arabic.

      References to the Koran, e.g. Koran 24:5 signify, chapter (Sura) 24, Statement (aya) 5.

2.   **The Bible. Revised Standard Version (1971) and Good News Bible.**
3.   **Hopfe, Lewis M. Religions of the World, fifth edition. Mc Millan Publishing C 1991.**

4.   **Jones, Baldick, Radice. Hindu Myths. The Penguin Classics 1975.**

5.   Wilson, William Julius. 1996. When Work Disappears. New York

6.   Naomi, Neft and Levine, Ann.D. 1997. Where Women Stand: An International Report on the Status of Women in 140 Countries. New York. Random House.

7.   Brotman, Barbara. 1000 Years. The Chicago Tribune. December 29, 1999 (Page 1, Section 8).

8.   Cairncross, John. 1974. After Polygamy was made a sin. London. Routledge & K.Paul.

9.   Ellerby, Helen. 1995. The Dark Side of Christian History. San Rafael. CA. Morningstar Books.

10.   Kamal, Omer. Deep into the Qur'an. 1989. Karachi, Pakistan

4

Sexuality and the Family

In the last four decades, the norms of our society have undergone vast changes in the area of premarital sexual permissiveness. Since the sexual revolution of the 1960s, society has become more permissive towards pre-marital sexual intercourse. Whereas the percentage of men engaging in premarital sex has remained stable throughout most of the last century, the percentage of women has increased tremendously, from 1 in 10 to 7 out of every 10 (Macionis 1987:543), bringing them at nearly the same percent as men.

The purpose of this chapter will be to theoretically and empirically examine the relationship between the attitude towards premarital sex (independent variable) and divorce (dependant variable).

The purpose of this research is to isolate and explain the "proximate cause" of the high divorce rate, which was observed in the decades after the 1960s. I argue that this "proximate cause" is the acceptance attitude towards premarital sex. It is like an "Irreducibly complex" system, similar to many biological systems. The blood clotting system in the human body works when a stimulus starts a chain [path] reaction of many enzymes and catalysts turning on and off in synchrony, automated to precision, leading to a common end. The isolated effect of the stimulus on a *particular* enzyme might not be very strong but the "contextual" effect is a necessary precondition. Therefore the stimulus can be termed as a direct cause of not only the intermediate mechanisms but also the final end. The Koran centuries back, described non–marital sex as a harmful "path" [*sabeel* in Arabic], leading to societal problems [Koran 17:9].

Theoretic Explanation:

The theoretical explanation of this analysis is found in several paradigms that operate at different levels of analysis. *Structural–Functionalism* regards regulation of sexual activity as one of the primary "functions" of the family. If you take this function away from the family, by liberalizing attitudes towards premarital sex (since nuclear families are formed via marriage), theory would predict a weaker family. Weaker families are more susceptible to divorce and being broken up.

If sex is legitimized outside of a marriage bond then one of the major reasons for getting married is taken away. The functions of a family complement the structure. The structure of a family is destabilized if the functions are taken away.

Structural Functionalism would predict dysfunctionality among broken families, due to a reduction in the "socialization pool" available to kids from such families. Lack of supervision among children of single–parent families and lack of a male role model makes them more susceptible to delinquency, normlessness and suicide (Hewlett 1991:104). Lack of adequate "learning" from a male model makes children relatively inadequately socialized in market activity (Biblarz & Raftery 1999). The Nuclear family performs certain functions in society which alternate family forms by "theoretic definition" would not be able to perform as effectively.

Axiom 1(a) *As the attitude towards premarital sex becomes (more) (+) permissive, the value of marriage as an institution weakens (–).*

Empirical Evidence: During the 1960s, society's strict disapproval of premarital sexual intercourse weakened under the so–called sexual revolution. Surveys carried out in the 1950s suggested that less than 25% of Americans endorsed premarital sex (ed. Edwards, Demo 1991). It should be mentioned that the attitude change concerning premarital sex precedes in time the attitude towards divorce. Premarital sex by definition takes place *before* marriage; divorce takes place *after* marriage. The attitude change towards premarital sex precedes in time the increase in the divorce rate that was observed in the United States in the 1970s. To establish causation, apart from correlation, the cause must precede the effect (Babbie 1992).

The changing norms were revealed by a 1979 college survey of 1300 students, 90% of those surveyed believed that it was acceptable to have sex with someone they loved regardless of marriage or legal commitment. In the sample, 77% of the men and 66% of the women had engaged in sexual intercourse premaritally (Derelga 1980).

As a result of this change in attitude, by the end of the 1980s, a U.S. Congress Report (1989) stated that most 19 year olds, 88% of men and 81% of women reported having premarital sex. Of those 15–19 (the 1965–1970 birth cohort), the incidence of premarital sex for men was 60% and that for women was 51.5% (Macionis 1987).

The increase in the number of people cohabiting and the attitude towards cohabitation:

With the increasing permissiveness towards premarital sex, and the resulting rise in the number of people engaging in premarital sex, delaying of marriage and lower age of premarital sexual experience, came a big increase in cohabitation, i.e. couples living together without a marriage bond and engaging in sexual activity. Since the 1970s, the number of cohabiting families increased 600% or six fold (Kornblum 1997). Data shows that a very large number of U.S. adults have cohabited at some point in their life since the attitude towards premarital sex changed. One third of adults in their mid–twenties and mid–thirties in the U.S. have cohabited before their first marriage, and over half of this age group has cohabited at "some point" in their lives (Smith 1999; Schaefer 2000;Brinkerhoff, White, Ortega 1999).

It is evident that society's increased acceptance towards premarital sex and the resulting increase in premarital sexual activity, especially among women, led to a breakdown of restricting norms associated with cohabitation. A study found that three–fourths of Americans over 65 oppose the practice of cohabitation (birth cohort of the pre 60s) while the numbers are reversed for those that are under thirty (Birth cohort of the 60s and 70s), i.e. three–fourth find nothing wrong with it (Ed.Edwards, Demo 1991).

Using the 1998 General Social Survey, a cross–tabulation between the questions, I) is premarital sex wrong? (*Premars1*) and II) Living together (cohabitation) as an acceptable option (*cohabok*)? [Both re–coded into dummy variables non–permissive [0]/permissive [1]], reveals in table 1, that of all those who are "non–permissive" regarding premarital sex, 83% are non–permissive towards cohabitation, compared to 16% of those that consider premarital sex "permissive". Only 17% of those that consider premarital sex "non–permissive" consider cohabitation "permissive" compared to 85% of those that consider premarital sex "permissive".

TABLE 1 The Relationship Between Cohabitation Permissiveness by Premarital Sexual Permissiveness	Respondent considers Premarital Sex Non-Permissive	Respondent Considers Premarital Sex Permissive
COHABITATION... Non-Permissive	331 83.4%	84 15.5%
COHABITATION... Permissive	66 16.6%	459 84.5%
TOTAL	397 100%	543 100%
Pearson chi-square 428.9, p< 0.001.		

A rise in the number of sexual partners: Before the breakdown of norms concerning premarital sex, marriage was more of an "only option" regarding sexual intercourse. Therefore, since sex partners were restricted to those maritally bonded, the number of sexual partners per person was lower than it is today. This delaying of marriage and increases in the number of years of exposure to premarital sex, led to the increase in the number of lifetime sexual partners that a person had. The number of women aged 15–19 in metropolitan areas, having two or more sexual partners increased from 38% in 1971 to 61% in 1988 (Smith 1998).

According to the 1993–1994 GSS, the married, averaged 0.97 partners. Those cohabiting had 1.38 partners and those who had never married had 1.63 (Smith 1998:4).

Using the data from the 1998 GSS (General Social Survey–University of Chicago), a cross–tabulation between the survey question, I) Is Premarital Sex Wrong? (Premars1) [Re–coded into non–permissive/permissive] and II) how many sex partners did you have last year? [Re–coded into 1 partner and 2 or more], confirms my conclusion in table 2. Of those who say that premarital sex is "non–permissive" only 6% have had two or more partners. However, among those who say that it is "permissive," 13% (double) have had two or more partners.

TABLE 2 The Relationship Between Number of Sex Partners by Premarital Sexual Permissiveness	Premarital Sex Non-Permissive	Premarital Sex Permissive
SEX PARTNERS... One only	450 94.1%	564 86.9%
SEX PARTNERS... Two or more	46 5.9%	147 13.1%
TOTAL	496 100%	711 100%
Pearson chi-square 28.27, p< 0.001.		

A rise in the number of the "Never–Married": A lowering of the importance of marriage in society was shown by a rising number of the never married. According to the *Information Please Almanac* (based on the US Census Bureau statistics), the never married are the fastest growing segment of adult population today in the U.S, and account for 23% of all adults *(Family Trends* 1997: 434). In 1970, 75% of adults were married; in the mid–1990s only 57% were married. From 1972 to 1996 those who had never been married rose from 15% to 22% (Smith 1998). In 1995, 67% of all women 20–24 years of age had never married compared to 36% in 1970 (Schaefer & Lamm 1998:401). Not only is marriage delayed, it is put off for good for a growing segment of the population.

A combination of this marital status variable that includes currently divorced and separated respondents and the variable "Ever been divorced or separated"; a dummy variable for divorce "DI" was constructed. The variable gives a score of 1 to those who are divorced or have ever been divorced and a score of 0 to all other categories. A cross tabulation between "DI" by premarital sexual permissiveness shows that of those that consider premarital sex "non–permissive" 27.4% have been divorced or are divorced (and separated) while 35% of those that consider it permissive have been or are divorced or separated. A difference of 8%

Table 3a The Relationship Between Divorce by Premarital Sexual Permissiveness	Premarital Sex Non-Permissive	Premarital Sex Permissive
Not Divorced	360 72.6%	464 65.3%
Divorced	136 27.4%	247 34.7%
Pearson chi-square 7.228, p< 0.01. Total	496 100%	711 100%

Decline in the marriage rate: The marriage rate is based on the number of marriages per 1000 people. It has declined steadily in the United States since 1970. The 1990 rate of 9.8 marriages per thousand appears to be higher than the 8.5 recorded in 1960, however the figure includes remarriages which dramatically increased over the last few decades and now account for 40% of the marriage rate (Thompson & Hickey 1994). According to the 1998 GSS, out of all respondents who considered premarital sex "non–permissive", 54% were married while only 43% of those that considered premarital sex "permissive" were married (see Table 3 above).
According to Percell:

> *When sex becomes more acceptable outside the bonds of marriage, one of the major reasons for getting married is undermined, helping to contribute to a lower marriage rate (1990: 310).*

Decrease in post–partum marriages: In the 1950s before the wide scale acceptance of premarital sex, most pregnancies that preceded marriage resulted in the man who had impregnated the woman marrying her (over 51%). This has changed since the acceptance of premarital sex and cohabitation (Wilson 1996). By the 1990s less than 25% of women who conceived a child before marriage got married before the child's birth (Smith 1998:5).

According to the National Health and Social Life Survey (NHSLS), a survey of 3432 adults in 1992, conducted among those born from 1933–1942, 94% of women married their first sexual partner compared to only 35% of women born from 1963–1970 (Schaefer & Lamm 1998:56).

According to Tom Smith of the National Opinion Research Center of the University of Chicago (1998):

> *With the link between sexual activity and marriage breaking down, the connection between marriage and procreation has also lessened...(1998:5)*

Increase in childbearing outside of wedlock: The weakness of marriage as an institution also shows up with an increasing number of women "choosing" to have kids outside of marriage. Before the breakdown of norms regarding premarital sex, marriage was the only option to have kids, now it is just "one" of the options. Overall the percentage of childbearing outside of wedlock has increased from 5% in 1960 to 33% of all births, in 1994 (Smith 1998). A similar trend showed up in Great Britain, where births outside of marriage increased from 5% in 1960 to 34% in 1995, from 4% to 26% in Canada, from 6% to 37% in France (Smith 1998:5). Whites account for most of the new rate increase in births outside of wedlock, at present. From 1980 to 1992 births out of wedlock grew 54% nationally, 94% for whites and 9% for blacks (Wilson 1996).

Extramarital sex goes up: As the attitude towards premarital sex became more permissive, we observed that marriage was delayed, and premarital sexual activity increased, together with the number of lifetime sexual partners. The lesser value placed on marriage showed up in an increasing rate of "marital infidelity" or extramarital sex. People, more than before the shift in these norms, were having a harder time adjusting from a premarital pattern of multiple sexual partners to a monogamous pattern of marriage. Those aged 40–49 (the birth cohort of 1960) show an extramarital sex incidence of 21%, while those 50 and older (the birth cohort of pre 1960) shows a significant drop, which reaches 7% for those 70 or older (the pre 1940 birth cohort) (Smith 1998:7). Recent studies suggest that as many as 50% to 65% of both men and women have had an extramarital sexual relationship in the United States by age 40 (Brinkerhoff, White, Ortega 1999:263; ed Edwards, Demo 1991). It should be noted that independent (not related to this paper) empirical studies on extramarital sex carried out by many researchers and narrated in *The Journal of Sex Research* published by the Society for the Scientific study of Sex 19 (1983): 1–22 stated (cited in ed. Edwards, Demo 1991):

> "…. *Attitudinal research strongly supports premarital sexual permissiveness as the most significant correlate of Extramarital sexual*

permissiveness (EMSP)." Evidence in support of other predictors is tenuous."

Using the 1998 General Social Survey, a cross–tabulation between the question, I) Is Premarital Sex Wrong?[re–coded into non–permissive/per-missive]; and II) Have you had sex other than your spouse when married?, confirms the relationship in table 4. Out of all those who responded that they had had sex with another even when married [*evstray*], reveals that 12.7% of those that considered premarital sex "non–permissive" had had sex with another while married, compared to 24.6% of those that considered premarital sex "permissive". Thus, the more permissive a person is regarding premarital sex, the more likely that he/she will cheat on their spouse.

TABLE 4 The Relationship Between Having Sex While Married (Extramarital Sex) By Premarital Sexual Permissiveness		Premarital Sex Non-Permissive	Premarital Sex Permissive
HAD SEX WHILE MARRIED?	YES	49 12.7%	112 24.6%
	NO	338 87.3%	343 75.4%
Pearson chi-square 62.94, p<0.001.	*TOTAL*	387 100%	455 100%

Among European countries, a similar trend as the United States is wit-nessed. There is however a difference in degree or intensity. In Sweden where the norms regarding premarital sex are most permissive [extremely liberal], families are the weakest, and the marriage institution has almost become obsolete, as premarital sex became institutionalized (Macionis 1995:463).

The empirical evidence above is clear, in support of axiom 1(a): *As attitudes towards premarital sex became more permissive (+), the value of marriage as an institution weakened (–).*

Axiom1 (b): **As the value of marriage as an institution weakens (–), the attitude towards divorce, becomes (more) permissive (+).**

Empirical Evidence: As the attitude towards premarital sex became more permissive, it was observed that the median marriage age for men and women rose, the number of people engaging in premarital sex rose, the average number of sex partners per person rose, the number of cohabiting couples rose and the number of people who put off marriage for good rose, while the number of "post–partum" marriages fell. Thus the value of marriage as an institution weakened.

Therefore, as marriage became weak, the value placed on the permanence of marriage became weak as well. As a result the attitude towards divorce became more permissive. This permissiveness regarding the attitude towards divorce showed up in the pressure put on the legislature to enact "no–contest" divorce laws, thus making divorce easier. As a result in 1969 (concurrent with when societal attitudes towards premarital sexual intercourse became more permissive), California became the first state to begin "no–fault" divorce, and most other states followed suit (Hewlett 1991).

The fact that the legislature was under pressure to enact easier divorce laws is revealed by the fact that divorce was already on the rise before this law was enacted (Schaefer & Lamm 1998:400). Thus, there was great demand for making divorce easier.

As we observed above, cohabitation can be inferred as the weakening of the importance of marriage as an institution. Therefore we should see, according to axiom 1(b) that those that cohabit, do not consider marriage as important as those who do not cohabit. Therefore they should have a more permissive attitude towards divorce, compared to groups that do not cohabit. Empirical evidence confirms this conclusion. Divorce rate for those who have cohabited before marriage is higher than those who haven't cohabited before marriage by over 10% (Kornblum 1997). The good "trial marriages," preceding marriage that Bertrand Russell was advocating based on his philosophy have today been proved wrong and unstable. Cohabitation preceding marriage results in a weaker marriage and not a stronger marriage as divorce rates clearly show.

As is observed above, the lesser the value of marriage, the greater is the permissive attitude towards divorce.

Proposition deduced from Axioms 1(a) and 1 (b):

The permissive attitude towards premarital sex led to a weakening of the marriage institution (Axiom 1(a)) which led to a permissive attitude towards divorce (Axiom 1(b)).

Concluding Deduction:

> *As the attitude towards divorce becomes (more) permissive (+),*
> *the number of couples divorcing (# of divorces) goes up (+).*

As the attitude towards divorce became more permissive, there was pressure on the legislature to enact divorce laws that made divorce easier. Once divorce was made "legally" easier by the enacting of "no–contest" divorce laws, the numbers of marriages ending in divorce multiplied enormously, increasing unabated until recently. The large increase in the divorce rate since the 1960s is attributed by most modern sociologists to the permissive attitude towards divorce (Schaefer 2000,Brinkerhoff, White, Ortega 1999,Smith 1998, Kornblum 1997, Newman 1998).

The divorce rate more than doubled from 1960 to 1980, increasing from 9.2 divorces per year per thousand marriages to 22.6, a 246% increase (Smith 1998). The divorce rate in the United States increased over ten–fold since 1890. For every hundred new marriages, fifty–two marriages (existing) will end in divorce (Schaefer 2000, Hewlett 1991). Within three years 20% of all new marriages either end in annulment or divorce (Kornblum 1997). Experts estimate that the lifetime divorce probability, for any marriage initiated in the last decade is 50%

(Brinkerhoff, White, Ortega 1999). Half of all marriages initiated in the last decade will inevitably end in divorce (Kornblum 1997). Another similar trend has been the rise in two–parent (step) families. In 1980, 9% of all family households with children included a stepparent, by 1990 this figure tripled to 24% (Schaefer & Lamm1998: 399).

The Cycle of Poverty:

It can be argued that the permissive attitude towards premarital sex (+) led to an increase in teen pregnancy (+), which then led to an increase in single female–headed parenthood (+), which led to the "feminization of poverty"(+). Poverty [and the psychological effects of divorce and "fatherlessness"] led to lower education and economic attainment in children (–), which led to a greater predisposition to premarital sex (+), which led to further teen pregnancy (+) in a "cycle of poverty".

Empirical Evidence:

> "Young girls growing up in broken homes become single parents themselves (53% more likely than those in intact homes do) due to early sexual activity outside of marriage. They are 164% more likely to have a premarital birth and 111% more likely to have a child as a teenager. Studies find that they have a higher incidence of divorce, and a 92% greater chance of dissolving their own marriage and lack of sexual confidence and orgasmic satisfaction. Even when income is removed as a dependant variable, the same results show disruption of family by divorce, and "fatherlessness" producing these traits." (Blackenhorn 1996).

The 1997 Information Please Almanac states [based on US Census Bureau data]:

> "The girls born to adolescent moms are up to 83% more likely to become teenage moms themselves, 50% more likely to repeat a grade at school and 50% more likely to born at a low birth

weight. Teenage moms are twice as likely to be on welfare and over 70% drop out of high school." (Family Trends 1997:435).

One of the nation's leading family scholars, Urie Bronfenbrenner of Cornell University, concludes:

> *"Controlling for associated factors such as low income, children growing up in such [female–headed] households are at a greater risk for experiencing a variety of behavioral and educational problems, including extremes of hyperactivity or withdrawal, lack of attentiveness in the classroom, difficulty in deferring gratification, impaired academic achievement, school misbehavior, absenteeism, dropping out, involvement in socially alienated peer groups, and especially the so called 'teenage syndrome' of behaviors that tend to hang together–smoking, drinking, early and frequent sexual experience, and in more extreme cases, drugs, suicide, vandalism, violence and criminal acts." (as cited in Blackenhorn 1996:249).*

Logical Deduction:

1. The permissive attitude towards premarital sex (+) led to a larger number of teenagers engaging in premarital sex (+). Axiom 3 (a)

Empirical Evidence:

In 1970, 5% of women who were age 15 and 32% of age 17 were sexually experienced. By 1988 this had grown to 26% at age 15 and 51% at 17. These numbers show that the average age for the first premarital encounter has been falling as more women engage in premarital sex, with changing attitudes towards it (Smith 1998).

In 1989, out of wedlock births accounted for 93% of all births to females below the age of 15, 77% of all births for those 15–17. (Karger, Sotez 1994).

2. With more teenagers engaging in premarital sex (+), teenage pregnancy went up (+) [engaging in sex is a necessary pre–condition for pregnancy]. Axiom 3(b)

Empirical Evidence:

In 1989, out of wedlock births accounted for 93% of all births to females below the age of 15, 77% of all births for those 15–17. In the age group 20–24, 35% of all births were to unmarried couples. Overall 25% of all white births were to unmarried couples and 70% of all African American births. (Karger, Sotez 1994).

Therefore:

3. Thus [proposition 3(a) and 3(b)] the permissive attitude towards premarital sex (+) led to an increase in teenage pregnancy (+) &

4. An increase in teenage pregnancy (+) led to an increase in teenage single moms (+)–

5. An increase in teenage single moms (+) led to "feminization of poverty" (deduced above)(+).

REPETITION OF THE CYCLE:

6. Poverty (+) led to lower education attainment in children of single female parents (+)

7. Lower education (–), [coupled with the psychological effects of divorce and "fatherlessness"] leads to higher incidence of premarital sex (+)

What is ironic in the practice of premarital sex related to attitude today is that most of the post 1960 birth cohort, consider premarital sex "revolutionary," "cool," and "good." What they don't realize is that there is an almost universal acceptance of premarital sex among primitive people (Kinsey 1948 et.all).

Therefore there is nothing "advanced" about premarital sex. Data in 1998 suggests that extramarital relations are more likely to occur among the less educated also (Smith 1998). Support for easy divorce is also highest among those that are less educated (34 % according to the 1997 GSS) and low among those with high degrees (19%) (Smith 1997: 11).

8. Higher incidence of premarital sex (+) leads to higher teenage pregnancy (+)

9. Higher teenage pregnancy (+) repeats the "cycle of poverty" discussed above.

Application:

The conclusions of this research can be extremely helpful in formulating social policy to deal with the "feminization of poverty" and its various effects. The solution is simple: We need to address the cause of the problem and seek prevention rather than trying to cure the effects. Since informal controls against premarital sex have greatly passed away with the changing norms regarding premarital sex, some formal laws need to be enacted as social policy to discourage premarital sex and to seek social change.

As society is educated and norms change again, formal laws will help society deal with the problem during the transitory period by controlling the wide scale practice of premarital sex. Results are definitely possible. A voluntary reduction in the incidence of premarital sex was witnessed after AIDS was publicized as a threat:

> *"Of people reporting a change in sexual behavior, about 45% to 50% mentioned reducing their number of sexual partners, including having only one partner... (Smith 1998:13)*

Another good example would be the reduction in smoking and a change of norms concerning cigarette smoking in the United States. Jean Kilbourne (1999) writes:

"Since Massachusetts increased taxes on cigarettes and launched a massive aggressive anti–tobacco campaign in 1993, consumption of cigarettes has dropped 31%, the steepest decline in smoking rates in the nation. In Florida, smoking by middle school students dropped 19% since the state launched an aggressive anti–tobacco campaign. Several studies have documented that in California, which has the oldest such program nationwide, in the 1990s smoking has declined twice as fast…and the norms for cigarette smoking have changed dramatically in the past 20 years (Kilbourne 1999:300)"

Violence and Crimes against Women:

Theory:

As premarital sex became more permissive, more women engaged in premarital sex [and the sex industry was born] leading to an objectification of the image of women and changing roles, resulting in a greater incidence of crimes against women.

1. *As premarital sex became more permissive (+) more women engaged in premarital sex (+). Axiom 4(a).*

   As more women engaged in premarital sex, the sex industry and media was born which led to a new image of a woman,, the woman as an "object."

2. *As the image of women in society as "objects" grew and different roles evolved (i.e. women were viewed more as "sex objects" rather than "homemakers") crimes against women (domestic violence and rape) increased (+). Axiom 4(b)*

3. *Thus, as premarital sex became more permissive (+), crimes against women became more common (+). Proposition 4 logically deduced from axiom 4(a) and 4(b).*

Empirical Evidence:

Since society became more permissive towards premarital sex, the number of women engaging in premarital sex went up by a large number (as we saw above). A culture of sex developed in the United States, with a new kind of industry taking birth, the growing "sex industry." Now, more than ever, women were being viewed as objects, "play things" and "toys" in the hands of men. The advertising industry was fast to catch on. By presenting women's nudeness to sell everything from ballpoint pens to automobiles, they desensitized the public to viewing women as sex objects.

Women's status and respect in society plummeted, compared to the 1950s, and crimes against women and domestic violence went up. According to psychologists, once a group is dehumanized and "objectified" as a thing, it becomes very easy to use violence against it (Kilbourne 1999). Women were being dehumanized and "objectified," and being programmed to hate everything about themselves, by the media. Commercials and advertisements showed that every part of the female anatomy had to be given a new look in order to make it socially acceptable according to the "Barbie" image. What was truly amazing was the deceit by which women were programmed to believe that this was something that built status and that they were being "liberated." Women thus turned against themselves following the permissiveness of premarital sex. It is also interesting to note that most businesses displaying the "sexuality" of women, through the popular media and through their "respectable" trades, the "entertainment industry", are owned by men.

According to the conflict school (and now the feminist school), men control society and seek means to keep women in their subordinate position. It appears true in this case, where by clever tactics, society has convinced women that hating every part of their body gives them "status", that changing everything that is their true self is "liberating." Once the image of women as "object", whole or dismembered (as displayed in advertisements) was established, it became very easy for society to become violent against them. As expected, we saw a big escalation in rape and domestic violence. Studies find that over 60% of college women have been sexually assaulted after the age of 14. The rates of "reported rape" are at least five times lower than the real number of rapes in America according to a study funded by the United States Department of Health and Human Services (Newman 1998). One woman in three in the U.S will face an "attempted or completed" rape in her lifetime (Hayden 1984:216).

From 1976 to 1980, reported rape, which is 5 times lower than actual rape, according to some estimates, went up by 38% (Derelga 1980). The National Victim Center reports (as cited by the Information Please Almanac 1997) that over 700,000 women are raped annually in the U.S. Given that most rapes go unreported, the actual number is much higher. The fear of rape among women has taken the public domain away from them. Women in the United States live under informal controls on what time and which areas in this country they have access too. Those who are not prudent to take note of these controls, make it on the evening news or the newspaper as another statistic on the ever–increasing number of women that are assaulted and molested on our streets every minute of every day.

Society is so permissive of rape, due to the desensitization resulting from the media portrayal of women, that rape has the lowest conviction rate of any violent crime. Only one out of one hundred and fifty suspected rapists are ever found guilty. Rape has been termed an "All American Crime," as surveys show that it embodies traditional male characteristics of power, domination and control that are highly valued in society (Newman 1998:454). It is little wonder that Sociologists today, talk about a "rape culture"(Hayden 1984).

Cultural belief in society about rape is that over 50% of both males and females blame the woman as being responsible for the rape (Newman

1998:456). This would be a classic example of "false consciousness" in women according to conflict theory. Women have been so programmed by the controllers of society, men that they blame themselves for the crime against them, which is actually being caused by society's "objectification" of women *contextually* caused by the greater acceptance attitude towards premarital sex.

It would not be wrong to theorize that this permissive attitude, according to the conflict school of thought, was: (i) introduced by men, who (ii) were always engaging in premarital sex, even before the sexual revolution, (iii) to increase the number of women engaging in premarital sex, (iv) desensitizing and perpetuating it through the media, owned by men, (v) so that they could be made objects of pleasure for men and kept subordinate through the "feminization of poverty."

Data in the United States shows that 25 to 35 percent of girls are sexually abused, usually by men well known to them and a third of all the women who are killed, die at the hands of husbands or boyfriends (Kilbourne 1999:253).

Shallower Relationships:

1. *The permissiveness of premarital sex (+) led to greater individualism (via the breakup of the family as we saw earlier) (axiom 5(a)).*

2. *Individualism going up (+) led to shallower husband/wife & parent/child relationship (−) (axiom 5(b).*

3. *Thus, the greater permissiveness of premarital sex (through a contextual effect) led to shallower relationships in society (Proposition 5 logically deduced from axiom 5(a) and 5(b).*

Empirical Evidence:

As society became more permissive towards premarital sex and as more couples started cohabiting, the attitude towards divorce became more permissive and no fault divorce laws were enacted. As a result of this, the divorce rate jumped as we saw earlier. The epidemic of divorce that hit American society showed us that even the most intimate husband/wife and parent/child relationship has became weak in this society. No longer was marriage viewed as a relatively permanent bond as people rushed to divorce.

Cohabiting which was a relatively new "intimacy" fad (as revealed by the high numbers), gave us even more alarming numbers of "shallow" intimacy. Of all the cohabiting couples, most part ways within a year or marry (Smith 1998). Of those that marry, the percentage of divorce is over 10% higher than the extremely high national rate of divorce among non–cohabiting couples (Kornblum 1997).

Recent studies suggest that as many as 50% to 65% of both men and women have had an extramarital sexual relationship in the United States by age 40 (Brinkerhoff, White, Ortega 1999:263; ed Edwards, Demo 1991). Considering that most people in America claim that "love" is the basis of courtship (Schaefer 2000:298), the numbers show that "claimed love" has become selfish and self centered due to this changing attitude towards premarital sex (the contextual cause).

As we saw earlier, premarital sex breaks up marriages by making the institution of marriage weak. When families break up, most fathers do not meet their children. Most men have started regarding marriage as a package deal. Once the marriage is broken, contact with children is severed also. Three out of four children feel rejected by their father after divorce (Hewlett 1991). This shows that even the close parent/child relationship has become weak in this society as a result of the permissiveness towards premarital sex.

Over 60% of children in single parent families didn't receive any support from their absent father in 1989. Single mothers and their children received only $11 billion in child support from the missing fathers, instead of their entitlement of $30 billion (Karger, Stoez 1994:107). Does this not show a shallow and irresponsible parent–child relationship?

According to the *interactionist* school, the most expressive symptom of loss of long–term commitment is the huge number of women raising children by themselves (Brinkerhoff, White, Ortega 1999). As we saw earlier, the permissive attitude towards premarital sex led through 'intervening variables' to the huge jump in single parenthood, as the marriage institution became weak and marriage got separated from reproduction. Research data shows that the amount of "total contact time" between parent and child in the United States has fallen 40% in the last twenty–five years (Hewlett 1991:91).

Premarital sex and sexual happiness:

Marriage is seen as something that restricts freedom. However sociological research finds that:

i) Married couples have a greater incidence of sexual activity, than the never married or divorced. Activity and sexual pleasure is 25% to 300% greater among married couples compared to non–married people at various age levels (Smith 1998).

ii) Married people are "happier" in their sexual life than non–married people (the total "amount" of sex among married couples is greater also than non married couples) according to the National Health and Social Life Survey (NHSLS) (Schaeffer 2000: 29).

iii)Marriage reduces crime and juvenile delinquency according to crime analysts (Siegel 1994:69).

iv) Marriage reduces the incidence of domestic violence (Blackenhorn 1996).

v) Married couples with children have higher household wealth and income than divorced or single parents.

As society became more permissive towards premarital sex, we saw the number of women engaging in premarital sex increase by leaps and bounds. As a result, sexual dysfunction, described as a lack of interest in the enjoyment of sex, performance anxiety or inability to have an orgasm, increased. Therefore we saw that sex in a marriage results in greater happiness than "single sex." (According to NHSLH narrated above). A 1999 study narrated in the Journal of American Medical Association, considered the most comprehensive look at American sexual behavior since the Kinsey Report, stated that sexual dysfunction affects 43% of women and 31% of men. What was surprising was that this was not correlated with age and that the birth cohort of the pre 1960 period were less likely to report dissatisfaction or lack of interest than the post 1960 birth cohort (Kilbourne 1999:266).

Summary and Conclusion:

We observed that as the attitude towards premarital sex became more permissive, the value of marriage as an institution weakened and a culture of divorce developed in the US. This was inferred by:

"The increase in the number of people cohabiting and the permissive attitude towards cohabitation. Those who are permissive towards premarital sex are 67.9% more likely to be permissive towards cohabitation than those that are non–permissive towards premarital sex (See Table 1)

"The rise in the number of sexual partners, following the delaying of marriage and the increase in the number of years of "exposure" to premarital sex. Those who are permissive towards premarital sex are twice as likely to have two or more sex partners than those that consider premarital sex non–permissive.

Increase in extramarital sex through its link to the attitude towards premarital sex, showing a weaker marriage bond (See Table 4). Those who consider premarital sex permissive were twice as likely to have had sex with another while married than those who did not.

As the value of marriage fell, we saw that the attitude towards divorce became more permissive and the divorce rate went up. Those who consider premarital sex permissive were 7.3% more likely to be divorced than those that considered premarital sex non–permissive (see Table 3a).

Those who are permissive towards cohabitation, which is caused by permissiveness towards premarital sex, were almost 10% more likely to be divorced than those who considered cohabitation non–permissive.

TABLE 9 The Relationship Between Divorce By Cohabitation Permissiveness	Cohabitation Non-Permissive	Cohabitation Permissive
Not Divorced	310 75.6%	527 64.6%
Divorced	100 24.4%	289 35.4%
TOTAL	410 100%	816 100%
Pearson chi-square 15.316, p< 0.001		

Regression analysis (see appendix) confirmed the above conclusions.

◆ The results showed that as a person who is permissive towards premarital sex has a 7% greater chance of being divorced than one who is non–permissive (b=0.06549). The results were statistically significant (p<0.05).

◆ Adjusting for minority status and cohort (pre–1960 and post–1960), the relationship between premarital sexual permissiveness and divorce became even stronger. It showed that those who were permissive towards premarital sexual permissiveness were

11.2% more likely to be divorced than those who were non–permissive. The results were statistically significant (p<0.001).

◆ When providing a link for cohabitation permissiveness, to the adjustment, premarital sex became non–significant and the results showed that cohabitation permissiveness was strongly related to divorce. Those who consider cohabitation permissive were 16% more likely to be divorced than those that consider it non–permissive.

◆ When cohabitation permissiveness was regressed on premarital sexual permissiveness it showed that those who are permissive regarding premarital sex have a 56.9% greater chance of being permissive towards cohabitation. Thus the conclusion being that premarital sexual permissiveness results in cohabitation permissiveness which results in a greater incidence of divorce. Almost 12% of the variation in divorce was explained by the model containing cohabitation permissiveness (Step 3 in table in appendix).

It was confirmed that premarital sexual permissiveness is a "cause" of divorce through cohabitation permissiveness. Literature review and existing data research showed that by affecting other variable, premarital sexual permissiveness weakens the marriage institution and affects divorce through multiple paths.

Appendix:

i) *Incidence of premarital sex*: The percentage of people who respond that they have engaged in premarital sex.

ii) *Incidence of Divorce*: The number of reported divorces per year per thousand individuals. It can also be measured as a percentage (ratio) of all marriages in a period (usually a year).

iii) *Cohabitation*: couples living together, as a household, without a blood or marriage relationship. Cohabitation is measured as a percentage of all households in a society.

iv) Median Marriage age: The median age of first marriage for men and women.

v) Feminization of poverty: Poverty concentration based on sex. Concentration of poverty exclusively in a segment of the female population.

vi) Female–headed household: Contrary to the traditional nuclear family, this family form is headed by a woman [the mother] with her children. The father is absent in most cases. This type gets formed when couples divorce or when women choose to have children outside of marriage. It is measured as a percentage of total number of households.

vii) The nuclear family: A two–parent [male–female] household, related by marriage, plus their children. The percentage of nuclear families is measured as a percentage of total number of households in a society.

Marriage Rate: The number of reported marriages per year per thousand individuals.

Regression Analysis:

In progressive adjustment, *Step 1* (refer to table), gives the total association between premarital sexual permissiveness and divorce. *Step 2*, adjusts for confounders, *cohort* and *minority* status and gives the total effect (direct plus indirect) of premarital sexual permissiveness on income. *Step 3* adjusts for the link, cohabitation permissiveness and gives the direct effect of premarital sexual permissiveness on divorce. The indirect effect being explained by cohabitation permissiveness.

Divorce regressed on premarital sexual permissiveness with adjustment for cohort, minority and cohabitation permissiveness.

	Step 1		Step 2		Step 3	
	Metric	Standard	Metric	Standard	Metric	Standard
Premarital Sexual Permissiveness N= 1160	0.06549* (0.028)→Std.Error	0.069	0.112*** (0.027)	0.119	0.02372 (0.033)	0.025
Cohort N= 1160			-0.293*** (0.027)	-0.311	-0.309*** (0.027)	-0.329
Minority N=1160			-.01796 (0.033)	-0.015	0.177 (0.031)	0.233
Cohabitation Permissiveness N=1600					0.158*** (0.034)	0.162
Intercept	0.276		0.376		0.332	
R (squared)	0.005		0.101		0.118	

Divorce (dependant) N=1160
*** p<0.001
** p<0.01 **One Tailed Test**
* p<0.05

The table shows that in *Step 1*, the total association between premarital sexual permissiveness and divorce is positive. The results are statistically significant ($p < 0.05$). It shows that if a person is permissive regarding premarital sex he/she has a 7% greater chance of getting divorced than one that is non–permissive ($b = 0.0655$ on a 0 to 1 scale). See Figure 1 at end.

Adjusting for cohort and minority status, *Step 2* shows that the total effect of premarital sexual permissiveness on divorce is a stronger positive than the earlier association. The results are statistically significant ($p < 0.001$). They show that if a person is permissive regarding premarital sex, he/she has an 11.2% greater chance of getting divorced ($b = 0.112$ on a 0 to 1 scale) than one who is non–permissive.

In Step 3, when I adjusted for cohabitation permissiveness, the effect of premarital sexual permissiveness became statistically insignificant ($p > 0.05$) but it showed that cohabitation permissiveness affected divorce in a strong positive manner. The results were statistically significant ($p < 0.001$). They show that if a person is permissive regarding cohabitation, he/she has a 15.8% greater chance ($b = 0.158$ on a 0 to 1 scale) of getting divorced than one who is non–permissive, controlling for cohort, minority status and premarital sexual permissiveness. The effect of cohort was statistically significant ($p < 0.001$). It shows that the post 1960 cohorts have a lesser chance of being divorced than the pre 1960 cohort. A reason for this might be that when the divorce rate shot up initially, the post 1960 cohort was still too young to be married. The effect of minority status was statistically insignificant.

The conclusions are completely in line with my theoretical model. The model suggested an "irreducibly complex" causation. In the model premarital sexual permissiveness causes attitudes towards cohabitation to become permissive. In such a model premarital sexual permissiveness has a causal effect on cohabitation permissiveness.

Model

Premarital Sexual Permissiveness -→ Cohabitation Permissiveness -→ Value of marriage

goes down

⬇

Divorce

In order to demonstrate this empirically, I regressed cohabitation permissiveness on premarital sexual permissiveness. Since cohabitation permissiveness was a dichotomous dummy variable, I checked the probability
to make sure that OLS could be efficiently run. The probability of cohabitation permissiveness was 0.67 (816/1226). Since 0.2<probability of
dependant<0.8, OLS would give the same result as a logistic regression.
The results show that 34.8% of the variation in cohabitation permissiveness is explained by premarital sexual permissiveness. There is a strong
positive relationship between premarital sexual permissiveness and cohabitation permissiveness. Those who are permissive regarding premarital sex
have a 56.9% greater chance of being permissive towards cohabitation
than those that are non–permissive towards premarital sex (b=0.569 on a
0 to 1 scale). The results are statistically significant (p<0.001).

Cohabitation Permissiveness Regressed on Premarital Sexual Permissiveness

	Step 1	
	Metric	Standard
Premarital Sexual Permissiveness	0.569***	0.590
	(0.023)→Std.Error	
N= 1160		
Intercept		0.324
R-squared		0.348

Bibliography:

Babbie, Earl. The Practice of Social Research. 1992. Wadsworth Publishing Company.

Biblarz, Timothy J and Raftery, Adrian E 1999. *"Family Structure, Educational Attainment, and Socioeconomic Success: Rethinking the "Pathology of Matriarchy."* American Journal of Sociology 105:321–65.

Brinkerhoff, David; Lynn, White; Ortega, Suzanne. 1999. *Sociology.* New York: Wadsworth Publishing Company.

Blankenhorn, David. 1996. *Fatherless America*. New York: Harper Perennial.

Domestic Violence. 1999. Facts on the Web. Retrieved 10/5/'99 (http://www.famvi.com/dv_facts.htm).

Edwards, John and Demo, David. Ed. 1991. *Marriage and Family in Transition*. Needham Heights, Ma: Allyn and Bacon.

Hewlitt, Sylvia Ann.1991. *When the Bough Breaks: The Cost of Neglecting Our Children*. New York: Harper Collins.

Information Please Almanac. 1993. (*Family Trends*) New York: Houghton Mifflin & Co.

Information Please Almanac. 1997. (*Family Trends*) New York: Houghton Mifflin & Co.

Janda, Louis; Derelga, J. 1980. *Personal Adjustment: The Psychology of Everyday Life*. New York: Scott Foresman & Co.

Kilbourne, Jean. 1999. *Deadly Persuasion*. New York: The Free Press.

Karger, Howard; Stoez, Jacobs. 1994. *American Social Welfare Policy*. Longman Publishing Company.

Leone, Bruno, ed.1999. *Poverty, Opposing Viewpoints*. San Diego: Greenhaven Press.

Macionis. John J. 1987. *Sociology*. New Jersey: Prentice Hall.

Macionis. John J. 1995. *Sociology*. New Jersey: Prentice Hall.

Thompson, William E & Hickey, Joseph V. Society in Focus. 1994. New York. Harper Collins

The Koran. Translated from the Arabic [References to the Koran, eg 17:9 refer to Sura (chapter) 17, aya (statement) 9].

Kinsey, Alfred C., Pomeroy, Wardell B., and Martin, Clyde E. 1948. *Sexual Behavior in the Human Male*. Philadelphia: W.B. Saunders.

Kornblum, William. 1997. *Sociology in a Changing World*. Orlando, Fl: Harcourt Brace & Company.

Newman, David M. 1997. *Sociology*. Thousand Oaks, Ca: Pine Forge Press.

Nunez, Ralph da Costa. 1994. *The New Poverty: Homeless Families in America.* New York: Insight Books.

Robertson, Ian. 1988. *Sociology.* New York: Worth Publishers.

Snow, David; Anderson, Leon. 1993. *Down on their Luck.* Berkley: University of California Press.

Schaefer, Richard T. 2000. *Sociology: A Brief Introduction.* New York: McGraw–Hill Higher Education.

The Online Resource for Social Justice. 1999. *Salt of the Earth.* Retrieved Sept 20, 1999(*http://www.claret.org/~salt/stats/homeless/home.html*)

Seigel. Larry J; Sienna. Joseph J. 1994. *Juvenile Delinquency.* West Publishing Company.

Smith, Tom. 1998. *American Sexual Behavior.* National Opinion Research Center. University of Chicago (General Social Survey. Topic # 25).

Smith, Tom. 1997. *Changes in Families and Family Values.* National Opinion Research Center: University of Chicago (Report prepared for the National Italian American Foundation).

U.S Department of Justice (http://www.famui.com/deptjust.html).

Wilson, William Julius. 1996. *When Work Disappears.* New York: Alfred A.Knopf.

Wallace, Walter. The Logic of Science in Sociology. 1971. Aldine Atherton. Chicago, il.

Hayden, Delores. *Redesigning the American* Dream. Ch 8.

Ardener, Shirley. *Women and Space.* 1981. New York.

5

The Instrument of Oppression

"They ask you concerning INTOXICANTS (Alcohol and other Drugs)…Say: In them is great harm and some benefits for humankind. But the harm of them is much greater than their benefit." (Koran 2:219)

The Food and Drug Administration (FDA) in the United States, uses the criterion of the Koran, given in the above statement, when it tests any new innovative drug. If the harm or side effects of any drug are found to exceed their usefulness, they banned from further production and marketing. Alcohol is such a "drug." It is the most highly abused "drug" in the United States. Its harm far exceeds any benefits that it provides when used as a beverage. Therefore a call to outlaw alcohol and drugs on a community level, as the Koran suggests, is justified based on objective criteria, criteria routinely administered by the FDA.

Alcohol consumption in any amount leads to a physiological tendency to abuse it, based on its effect on the serotonin levels in the brain. Therefore, "responsible" drinking is itself an irresponsible idea. Therefore, the Koran's call to completely shun alcohol and other intoxicants is justified because law has to be applied uniformly.

For the law to be applied justly and uniformly, in order to benefit society as a whole, those who have a greater tendency to abuse alcohol shouldn't have access to the drug neither should those who have a lesser tendency to abuse it. Laws that are applied society–wide cannot discriminate between those with different tendencies to abuse a harmful substance. However, for the purpose of rehabilitation, the Koran allows the use of alcohol based on its principle of dietary laws being flexible in order to save lives, *"without willful transgression."(Koran 2:174)*

Alcohol is harmful on an individual and a social level:

1. 60–70% of all crime involves alcohol and/or other intoxicating drugs. Almost 50% of all violent crimes involve alcohol. Twenty–four percent of Federal inmates and 49% of State inmates reported that they were under the influence of alcohol or illicit drugs at the time of their current offense. 36.3% were under the influence of alcohol alone. Federal research also shows that more than 40% of convicted murderers being held in jail or State prison, had alcohol as a factor in their crime.

   Extensive data is available to show the relationship between violent crime and alcohol. In the United Kingdom, the British Medical Association, advised the Parliament that alcohol is a factor in:
   - 60–70% of homicides
   - 75% of stabbings
   - 70% of beatings
   - 50% of fights and domestic assaults.

   According to the Seventh Special Report to the U.S Congress on Alcohol and Health, *"In both animal and human studies, alcohol more than any other drug, has been linked with a high incidence of violence and aggression."*

   Alcohol temporarily increases brain serotonin function, but after that temporary rise, levels of serotonin fall below the normal level. This reduced serotonin level is linked to a heightened vulnerability to depression, increased risk of violent suicide, aggressive and impulsive behavior, and a tendency to further abuse alcohol, according to the National Institute on Drug Abuse (NIDA). Alcohol consumption in any amount leads biologically (through serotonin) to a tendency to abuse it. There is no such thing as "responsible" drinking on a society–wide level.

"...Alcohol, the oldest and most prevalent cause of addiction, is by far the most prolific activator and deactivator of brain centers. Nothing else comes close. Not cocaine, not heroin, not nicotine... Using PET scanners, University of Chicago scientists studied the effects of alcohol on the brain. Since alcohol affects the pleasure centers of the brain (the limbic network in the mid brain), it is directly responsible for compulsion, addiction and craving." (Kotulak 1997:111)

"But to modern scientists, the discovery of alcohol's ability to turn on the brain's reward system is the key to understanding how alcohol creates a craving so intense that it makes emotion rule over reason. When a person slips into dependence, alcohol craving becomes a drive as powerful as the need for food, water, sleep and sex."(Kotulak 1997:116)

2) Nearly 50% of Automobile fatalities in the U.S. are linked to Alcohol (one death every 11 minutes according to 1990 estimates). Forty percent of all fatal motor vehicle crashes involve alcohol. Drunk driving is the nation's most frequently committed violent act. In 1990, 22,083 people died in car accidents involving alcohol. This is equivalent to three fully loaded 747s crashing three times a week, every week for a year. About two in every five Americans will be involved in an alcohol–related car crash sometimes in their lives. (http://www.geocities.com/Heartland/Plains/3121/statistics.html).

3) Fetal Alcohol Syndrome (FAS) results in mental and physical retardation of the newborn. The incidence of FAS in the United States is 1.9 cases per every 1000 births. Birth defects other than FAS linked to alcohol use are 1 in every 100 births. Statistically these numbers

are huge. According to the World Health Organization (WHO), the net rates for FAS are 1 in 500 for US, Canada, Europe and Australia combined. In 1991, The Journal of the American Medical Association (JAMA) reported that FAS (Fetal Alcohol Syndrome) is the leading known cause of mental retardation in Western Civilization (see http://come–over.to/FAS)

4) As many as half the young offenders appearing in provincial court may be there because their mothers drank (alcohol) during pregnancy, says Royal University Hospital psychologist Josephine Nanson. (See, http://www.treefort.org/~tjk/fas/zakreski.htm).

5) Almost 78% of all assaults, most of them involving men beating women, are committed under the influence of alcohol. In the United States, a man beats a woman every 15 seconds. Two–thirds (75%) of partner abuse victims in the US report that alcohol had been a factor. For spouse abuse victims, the offender was drinking three out of four times (See, http://www.tf.org/alcohol/ariv/reviews/dvrev5.html)

6) Alcohol causes permanent damage to the brain, liver and most internal organs of the consumer. It is a poison, which the body tries to get rid of the moment it is consumed. An enzyme in the stomach, alcohol dehydrogenase, tries to neutralize the ethanol content in alcoholic beverages, treating it as a poison.

Since women have a higher proportion of body fat and less water in their bodies, this means that alcohol will be less diluted and have a greater effect on them compared to men. Also, the enzyme in the stomach that neutralizes ethanol, alcohol dehydrogenase, in women is 70–80% less effective than it is in men. Alcohol, therefore, causes even greater harm to women. In women that drink heavily, cirrhosis of the liver sets in within 13 years compared to the 22 years for men (see http://www.alcohol.or/nz).

7) Alcohol acts as a "stepping–stone" for other "higher" drugs like Marijuana, Cocaine and Heroine. Those who don't do alcohol don't experiment with other drugs (Siegel, Sienna 1994). This is in contrast to "stimulants" like caffeine, which don't figure out in this "stepping stone". According to the National Institute on Drug Abuse (NIDA), treatment data suggests, *"Increasing proportions of persons treated for alcohol problems also have drug problems."* Thus, the "drug war" can never be won without outlawing alcohol.

8) According to NIDA, the economic cost to society of alcohol was estimated at $148 billion in 1992. When adjusted for inflation and population growth, the cost increases over 12.5% every year. (See http://www.nida.nih.gov/EconomicCosts/Index.html).

Recently, the alcohol industry started a new marketing scam, encouraging alcohol use as being beneficial to health. The contingencies involved in such negligible "benefits" that were advertised with "passion" are such that these benefits have not accrued on aggregate levels at all. We haven't seen deaths related to heart disease go down since these "benefits" were advertised, in the United States, because of alcohol use. What we see is that deaths directly related to alcohol, are high in every country where alcohol is part of the culture (Weeks 2000). We can conclude therefore that the harms of alcohol far exceed any benefits that it has when used as a beverage.

> *"A great deal of publicity has been given to the beneficial effects of red wine[11] in keeping heart disease rates lower in France than in the United States, but closer inspection of death rates suggests that red wine has not protected the French against other causes of death (related to alcohol), ...10% of all deaths in France are*

---

[11] According to a study published in the American Journal of Clinical Nutrition, removing the alcohol content of red wine does not reduce its health–giving properties but may actually increase them (as reported in the BBC News, Health 30 December 1999).

traceable to alcohol consumption (higher than that in the US)[12]." (Weeks 2000:126–127)

Jean Kilbourne (1999) effectively summarizes the ironies involved with alcohol use in Western culture. The description unmasks the nature of this instrument of oppression and its effective use to trap the masses:

" In the case of alcohol, we drink to feel glamorous and sophisticated, and often end up staggering, vomiting, and screaming. We drink to feel courageous and are overwhelmed by fear and a sense of impeding doom. We drink to have better sex, but alcohol eventually makes most of us sexually dysfunctional. We do this to ourselves because of our disease, but we also do it in a cultural climate in which people who understand the nature of our disease,surround us with powerful images, associating alcohol with glamour, courage, sexiness and love, precisely what we need to believe in order to stay in denial.

Above all, we drink to feel connected and, in the process we destroy all possibility of real intimacy and end up profoundly isolated..."(Kilbourne 1999:250)

Sources:

Asadi, Muhammed. *Alcohol: The Instrument of Oppression.* (*http://www.geocities.com/justiceparadigm/alcohol.htm*)

Kilbourne, Jean. *Deadly Persuasion.* 1999. The Free Press.

Kotulak, Ronald. *Inside the Brain: Revolutionary Discoveries of how the mind works.* 1997. Andrews & Mcmeal

Weeks, Robert J. Population: An introduction to concepts and issues. 2000. Wadsworth Publishing Company.

---

[12] In the US, around 110,000 deaths per year are attributed to alcohol

The Justice Paradigm

In concluding this analysis, a short nine point "ideal type", directly quoted from the Koran, is presented. When translated into the macro, it is the essence of the Justice Paradigm:

"Sincere servers of the Merciful God are those:

1. *Who walk upon the earth modestly, and when the foolish address them they answer "Peace".*

2. *Who spend the night before God standing and in prostration (in self–evaluation).*

3. *Who when they spend (on themselves and in God's way), are neither prodigal nor grudging, but seek a just stand between the two.*

4. *Who submit not to any other except God, neither take life that God has forbidden, except where justice requires; neither commit non–marital sex–Whoever does these will pay the penalty...*

5. *Except, the ones who i) repent, ii) affirms the truth, iii) and do what is right and remedial (Saaleh in Arabic); as for such God will change their wrong into good. Indeed God is Forgiving, Merciful.*

6. *Whoever repents and does good, repents to God with sincerity.*

7. *Who do not attest or witness to falsehood, and maintain their dignity when around senselessness.*

8. *Those who when they are reminded of God's revelations (reason about them) and do not fall on them deaf and blind.*

9. *And those who say: "My God! Provide for us mates and children, such as are a comfort to the eyes, and make us as standards for those who are socially aware.*

   These are the ones that will be awarded with the high places for they were steadfast and they will be met with welcome and peace..." (Koran 25:63–74)

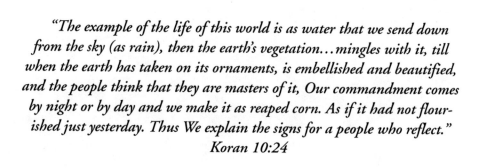

"*The example of the life of this world is as water that we send down from the sky (as rain), then the earth's vegetation…mingles with it, till when the earth has taken on its ornaments, is embellished and beautified, and the people think that they are masters of it, Our commandment comes by night or by day and we make it as reaped corn. As if it had not flourished just yesterday. Thus We explain the signs for a people who reflect.*"
Koran 10:24

0-595-20896-7

LaVergne, TN USA
06 August 2010
192328LV00003B/88/A